FIX-IT and FORGET-IT®

HEALTHY
5-Ingredient
COOKBOOK

150 EASY AND NUTRITIOUS SLOW COOKER RECIPES

HOPE COMERFORD

Photos by Bonnie Matthews

Good Books

New York, New York

To my beautiful and smart friend, "sister," and confidant, Andrea.
Thank you for teaching me what being truly healthy is!

Table of Contents

Welcome to Fix-It and Forget-It Healthy 5-Ingredient Cookbook

Eating healthy doesn't have to be hard, and we're here to prove it to you! It's all in the ingredients you use. You'll find this book to be full of recipes you can feel good about eating! With step-by-step instructions and common ingredients, you'll be feeling like a pro in the kitchen in no time.

This book is divided into six different sections for you: Breakfasts; Appetizers and Snacks; Soups, Stews, and Chilies; Main Dishes; Side Dishes and Vegetables; and Desserts and Beverages. You know the word "desserts" got your attention! That's right! There are even healthy desserts! For every recipe, we've included nutritional information to further help you with your dietary needs.

If you find a recipe you love, but it calls for an ingredient you can't have, please feel free to sub it with one that fits your particular allergen or dietary needs. For instance, if a recipe calls for peanut butter, but you have a peanut allergy, feel free to sub that with sun butter. Or, if a recipe calls for gluten-free soy sauce and you do not have a gluten-allergy or sensitivity, feel free to use regular soy-sauce. It's easy to make a recipe work for you! Most of the recipes in this book can be very easily adjusted!

What qualifies as a 5-Ingredient recipe?

- A recipe that has 5 or fewer ingredients.
- Spices do not count.
- Water does not count.
- *Optional* ingredients do not count.
- Serving suggestion items, such as rice or pasta, do not count.

Choosing a Slow Cooker

Not all slow cookers are created equal . . . or work equally well for everyone!

Those of us who use slow cookers frequently know we have our own preferences when it comes to which slow cooker we choose to use. For instance, I love my programmable slow cooker, but there are many programmable slow cookers I've tried that I've strongly disliked. Why? Because some go by increments of 15 or 30 minutes and some go by 4, 6, 8, or 10 hours. I dislike those restrictions, but I have family and friends who don't mind them at all! I am also pretty brand loyal when it comes to my manual slow cookers, because I've had great success with those and have had unsuccessful moments with slow cookers of other brands. So, which slow cooker(s) is/are best for your household?

It really depends on how many people you're feeding and if you're gone for long periods of time. Here are my recommendations:

For 2–3 person household	3–5 quart slow cooker
For 4–5 person household	5–6 quart slow cooker
For a 6+ person household	6½–7 quart slow cooker

Large slow cooker advantages/disadvantages:

Advantages:
- You can fit a loaf pan or a baking dish into a 6- or 7-quart, depending on the shape of your cooker. That allows you to make bread or cakes, or even smaller quantities of main dishes. (Take your favorite baking dish and loaf pan along when you shop for a cooker to make sure they'll fit inside.)
- You can feed large groups of people, or make larger quantities of food, allowing for leftovers, or meals, to freeze.

Disadvantages:
- They take up more storage room.
- They don't fit as neatly into a dishwasher.
- If your crock isn't ⅔–¾ full, you may burn your food.

Small slow cooker advantages/disadvantages:

Advantages:
- They're great for lots of appetizers, for serving hot drinks, for baking cakes straight in the crock, and for dorm rooms or apartments.
- Great option for making recipes of smaller quantities.

Disadvantages:
- Food in smaller quantities tends to cook more quickly than larger amounts. So keep an eye on it.
- Chances are, you won't have many leftovers. So, if you like to have leftovers, a smaller slow cooker may not be a good option for you.

My recommendation:

Have at least two slow cookers; one around 3 to 4 quarts and one 6 quarts or larger. A third would be a huge bonus (and a great advantage to your cooking repertoire!). The advantage of having at least a couple is you can make a larger variety of recipes. Also, you can make at least two or three dishes at once for a whole meal.

Manual vs. Programmable

If you are gone for only six to eight hours a day, a manual slow cooker might be just fine for you. If you are gone for more than eight hours during the day, I would highly recommend purchasing a programmable slow cooker that will switch to warm when the cook time you set is up. It will allow you to cook a wider variety of recipes.

The two I use most frequently are my 4-quart manual slow cooker and my 6½-quart programmable slow cooker. I like that I can make smaller portions in my 4-quart slow cooker on days I don't need or want leftovers, but I also love how my 6½-quart slow cooker can accommodate whole chickens, turkey breasts, hams, or big batches of soups. I use them both often.

Get to know your slow cooker . . .

Plan a little time to get acquainted with your slow cooker. Each slow cooker has its own personality—just like your oven (and your car). Plus, many new slow cookers cook hotter and faster than earlier models. I think that with all of the concern for food safety, the slow-cooker manufacturers have amped up their settings so that "High," "Low," and "Warm" are all higher temperatures than in the older models. That means they cook hotter—and therefore, faster—than the first slow cookers. The beauty of these little machines is that they're supposed to cook low and slow. We count on that when we flip the switch in the morning before we leave the house for ten hours or so. So, because none of us knows what kind of temperament our slow cooker has until we try it out, nor how hot it cooks—don't assume anything. Save yourself a disappointment and make the first recipe in your new slow cooker on a day when you're at home. Cook it for the shortest amount of time the recipe calls for. Then, check the food to see if it's done. Or if you start smelling food that seems to be finished, turn off the cooker and rescue your food.

Also, all slow cookers seem to have a "hot spot," which is of great importance to know, especially when baking with your slow cooker. This spot may tend to burn food in that area if you're not careful. If you're baking directly in your slow cooker, I recommend covering the "hot spot" with some foil.

Take notes . . .

Don't be afraid to make notes in your cookbook. It's yours! Chances are, it will eventually get passed down to someone in your family, and they will love and appreciate all of your musings. Take note of which slow cooker you used and exactly how long it took to cook the recipe. The next time you make it, you won't need to try to remember. Apply what you learned to the next recipes you make in your cooker. If another recipe says it needs to cook 7–9 hours, and you've discovered your slow cooker cooks on the faster side, cook that recipe for 6–6½ hours and then check it. You can always cook a recipe longer—but you can't reverse things if it's overdone.

Get creative . . .

If you know your morning is going to be hectic, prepare everything the night before, take it out so the crock warms up to room temperature when you first get up in the morning, then plug it in and turn it on as you're leaving the house.

If you want to make something that has a short cook time and you're going to be gone longer than that, cook it the night before and refrigerate it for the next day. Warm it up when you get home. Or, cook those recipes on the weekend when you know you'll be home and eat them later in the week.

Slow Cooking Tips and Tricks and Other Things You May Not Know

- Slow cookers tend to work best when they're ⅔ to ¾ of the way full. You may need to increase the cooking time if you've exceeded that amount, or reduce it if you've put in less than that. If you're going to exceed that limit, it would be best to reduce the recipe, or split it between two slow cookers. (Remember how I suggested owning at least two or three slow cookers?)

- Keep your veggies on the bottom. That puts them in more direct contact with the heat. The fuller your slow cooker, the longer it will take its contents to cook. Also, the more densely packed the cooker's contents are, the longer they will take to cook. And finally, the larger the chunks of meat or vegetables, the more time they will need to cook.

- Keep the lid on! Every time you take a peek, you lose 20 minutes of cooking time. Please take this into consideration each time you lift the lid! I know, some of you can't help yourself and are going to lift anyway. Just don't forget to tack on 20 minutes to your cook time for each time you peeked!

- Sometimes it's beneficial to remove the lid. If you'd like your dish to thicken a bit, take the lid off during the last half hour to hour of cooking time.

- If you have a big slow cooker (7- to 8-quart), you can cook a small batch in it by putting the recipe ingredients into an oven-safe baking dish or baking pan and then placing that into the cooker's crock. First, put a trivet or some metal jar rings on the bottom of the crock, and then set your dish or pan on top of them. Or a loaf pan may "hook on to" the top ridges of the crock belonging to a large oval cooker and hang there straight and securely, "baking" a cake or quick bread. Cover the cooker and flip it on.

- The outside of your slow cooker will be hot! Please remember to keep it out of reach of children and keep that in mind for yourself as well!

- Get yourself a quick-read meat thermometer and use it! This helps remove the question of whether or not your meat is fully cooked, and helps prevent you from overcooking your meat as well.

  Internal Cooking Temperatures:
  - Beef—125–130°F (rare); 140–145°F (medium); 160°F (well-done)
  - Pork—140–145°F (rare); 145–150°F (medium); 160°F (well-done)
  - Turkey and Chicken—165°F

- Frozen meat: The basic rule of thumb is, don't put frozen meat into the slow cooker. The meat does not reach the proper internal temperature in time. This especially applies to thick cuts of meat! Proceed with caution!
- Add fresh herbs 10 minutes before the end of the cooking time to maximize their flavor.
- If your recipe calls for cooked pasta, add it 10 minutes before the end of the cooking time if the cooker is on High; 30 minutes before the end of the cooking time if it's on Low. Then the pasta won't get mushy.
- If your recipe calls for sour cream or cream, stir it in 5 minutes before the end of the cooking time. You want it to heat but not boil or simmer.

Approximate Slow Cooker Temperatures (Remember, each slow cooker is different):
- High—212°F–300°F
- Low—170°F–200°F
- Simmer—185°F
- Warm—165°F

Cooked and dried bean measurements:
- 16-oz. can, drained = about 1¾ cups beans
- 19-oz. can, drained = about 2 cups beans
- 1 lb. dried beans (about 2½ cups) = 5 cups cooked beans

Breakfasts

Breakfast Sausage Casserole

Kendra Dreps, Liberty, PA

Makes 8 servings
Prep Time: 15 minutes ♣ Chilling Time: 8 hours ♣ Cooking Time: 4 hours ♣ Ideal slow cooker size: 3-qt.

1 lb. loose turkey sausage

6 eggs

2 cups unsweetened almond milk

8 slices whole-grain or sprouted-grain bread, cubed

2 cups reduced-fat shredded cheddar cheese

1. In a nonstick skillet, brown and drain sausage.

2. Mix together eggs and milk in a large bowl.

3. Stir in bread cubes, cheese, and sausage.

4. Place in a greased slow cooker.

5. Refrigerate overnight.

6. Cook on Low 4 hours.

Variation:

Use cubed cooked ham instead of sausage.

Cal: 250
Fat: 12g
Sodium: 560mg
Carbs: 13g
Sugar: 1g
Protein: 23g

Breakfast Bake

Kristi See, Weskan, KS

Makes 10 servings
Prep Time: 15 minutes ♣ Cooking Time: 3–4 hours ♣ Ideal slow-cooker size: 4- to 5-qt.

12 eggs

1½–2 cups grated reduced-fat cheese, your choice

1 cup diced cooked ham

1 cup unsweetened almond milk

1 tsp. sea salt

½ tsp. pepper

1. Beat eggs. Pour into the slow cooker.

2. Mix in remaining ingredients.

3. Cover and cook on Low 3–4 hours.

Cal: 120
Fat: 8g
Sodium: 460mg
Carbs: 1g
Sugar: 0g
Protein: 11g

Huevos Rancheros in Crock

Pat Bishop, Bedminster, PA

Makes 6 servings

Prep Time: 25 minutes ☙ Cooking Time: 2 hours ☙ Ideal slow-cooker size: 6-qt.

3 cups gluten-free salsa, room temperature

2 cups cooked beans, drained, room temperature

6 eggs, room temperature

salt and pepper to taste

⅓ cup reduced-fat grated Mexican-blend cheese, *optional*

1. Mix salsa and beans in the slow cooker.

2. Cook on High for 1 hour or until steaming.

3. With a spoon, make 6 evenly spaced dents in the salsa mixture; try not to expose the bottom of the crock. Break an egg into each dent.

4. Salt and pepper eggs. Sprinkle with cheese if you wish.

5. Cover and continue to cook on High until egg whites are set and yolks are as firm as you like them, approximately 20–40 minutes.

6. To serve, scoop out an egg with some beans and salsa.

Serving Suggestion:

Serve with warm white corn tortillas.

Calories: 200
Fat: 1g
Sodium: 975mg
Carbs: 36g
Sugar: 6g
Protein: 12g

Spinach Fritatta

Shirley Unternahrer, Wayland, IA

Makes 4–6 servings
Prep Time: 15 minutes & *Cooking Time: 1½–2 hours* & *Ideal slow-cooker size: 5-qt.*

4 eggs

½ tsp. kosher salt

½ tsp. dried basil

fresh ground pepper, to taste

3 cups chopped fresh spinach, stems removed

½ cup chopped tomato, liquid drained off

⅓ cup freshly grated Parmesan cheese

1. Whisk eggs well in mixing bowl. Whisk in salt, basil, and pepper.

2. Gently stir in spinach, tomato, and Parmesan.

3. Pour into lightly greased slow cooker.

4. Cover and cook on High for 1½–2 hours, until middle is set. Serve hot.

TIP

This is a great dish when you have company for breakfast. No last-minute preparation needed!

Calories: 90

Fat: 5.5g

Sodium: 420mg

Carbs: 3g

Sugar: .5g

Protein: 7g

Crustless Spinach Quiche

Barbara Hoover, Landisville, PA

Makes 8 servings
Prep Time: 15 minutes & Cooking Time: 2–4 hours & Ideal slow-cooker size: 3- or 4-qt.

2 10-oz. pkgs. frozen chopped spinach

2 cups cottage cheese

¼ cup coconut oil

1½ cups reduced-fat sharp cheddar cheese, cubed

3 eggs, beaten

¼ cup all-purpose gluten-free flour, *optional*

1 tsp. salt

1. Grease interior of slow-cooker crock.

2. Thaw spinach completely. Squeeze as dry as you can. Then place in crock.

3. Stir in all other ingredients and combine well.

4. Cover. Cook on Low 2–4 hours, or until quiche is set. Stick blade of knife into center of quiche. If blade comes out clean, quiche is set. If it doesn't, cover and cook another 15 minutes or so.

5. When cooked, allow to stand 10–15 minutes so mixture can firm up. Then serve.

Calories: 250
Fat: 18.5g
Sodium: 675mg
Carbs: 7.5g
Sugar: 2.5g
Protein: 15.5g

Slow-cooker Oatmeal

Martha Bender, New Paris, IN

Makes 7–8 servings
Prep Time: 10–15 minutes ♣ *Cooking Time: 8–9 hours* ♣ *Ideal slow-cooker size: 4- to 5-qt.*

2 cups gluten-free rolled oats
4 cups water
I large apple, peeled and chopped
I cup raisins
I tsp. cinnamon
I–2 Tbsp. orange zest

1. Combine all ingredients in your slow cooker.

2. Cover and cook on Low 8–9 hours.

3. Serve topped with brown sugar, if you wish, and milk.

Cal: 80
Fat: 1g
Sodium: 0mg
Carbs: 17g
Sugar: 7g
Protein: 2g

Breakfast Oatmeal

Donna Conto, Saylorsburg, PA

Makes 6 servings
Prep Time: 5 minutes ☙ Cooking Time: 8 hours ☙ Ideal slow-cooker size: 4-qt.

2 cups dry gluten-free rolled oats

4 cups water

1 tsp. sea salt

½–1 cup chopped dates, raisins, or cranberries, or a mixture of any of these fruits

1. Combine all ingredients in the slow cooker.

2. Cover and cook on Low overnight, or for 8 hours.

TIP
This is a great dish when you have company for breakfast. No last-minute preparation needed!

Cal: 170
Fat: 2g
Sodium: 380mg
Carbs: 37g
Sugar: 15g
Protein: 4g

Overnight Oatmeal

Jody Moore, Pendleton, IN

Makes 4–5 servings
Prep Time: 5 minutes ⚶ *Cooking Time: 8 hours* ⚶ *Ideal slow-cooker size: 3-qt.*

I cup dry gluten-free steel cut oats

4 cups water

1. Combine ingredients in the slow cooker.

2. Cover and cook on Low overnight, or for 8 hours.

3. Stir before serving. Serve with brown sugar, ground cinnamon, fruit preserves, jam, jelly, pumpkin-pie spice, fresh fruit, maple syrup, or your other favorite toppings.

TIP

Please note that steel cut oats are called for. They are different—with more texture, requiring a longer cooking time—than old-fashioned or rolled oatmeal.

Cal: 120
Fat: 2g
Sodium: 10mg
Carbs: 22g
Sugar: 1g
Protein: 4g

Oatmeal Morning

Barbara Forrester Landis, Lititz, PA

Makes 6 servings
Prep Time: 10 minutes ⚘ *Cooking Time: 2½–6 hours* ⚘ *Ideal slow-cooker size: 3-qt.*

1 cup uncooked gluten-free steel cut oats

1 cup dried cranberries

1 cup walnuts

½ tsp. kosher salt

1 Tbsp. cinnamon

2 cups water

2 cups fat-free nondairy milk (almond, rice, etc.)

1. Combine all dry ingredients in the slow cooker. Stir well.

2. Add water and milk and stir.

3. Cover. Cook on High 2½ hours, or on Low 5–6 hours.

Calories: 260
Fat: 12g
Sodium: 215mg
Carbs: 38g
Sugar: 14g
Protein: 6g

German Chocolate Oatmeal

Hope Comerford, Clinton Township, MI

Makes 4 servings
Prep Time: 5 minutes ❧ *Cooking Time: 6–8 hours* ❧ *Ideal slow-cooker size: 3-qt.*

2 cups gluten-free steel cut oats

8 cups unsweetened coconut milk

¼ cup unsweetened cocoa powder

¼ tsp. kosher salt

brown sugar, *optional*

sweetened shredded coconut (enough for a sprinkle on top of each bowl)

1. Spray crock with nonstick spray.

2. Place steel cut oats, coconut milk, cocoa powder, and salt into crock and stir to mix.

3. Cover and cook on Low for 6–8 hours.

4. To serve, top each bowl of oatmeal with desired amount of brown sugar, if desired, and a sprinkle of shredded coconut.

Cal: 519
Fat: 11g
Sodium: 425mg
Carbs: 91g
Sugar: 19g
Protein: 13g

Overnight Oat Groats

Rebekah Zehr, Lowville, NY

Makes 6 servings
Prep Time: 5 minutes & *Cooking Time: 8–10 hours* & *Ideal slow-cooker size: 3-qt.*

1½ cups gluten-free oat groats

4 cups water

2 cups almond milk

1–2 cinnamon sticks

⅓ cup maple syrup

½–1 cup dried apples

2 scoops gluten-free vanilla-flavored protein powder, *optional*

1. Combine all ingredients in the slow cooker.

2. Cook on Low for 8–10 hours.

3. Remove cinnamon sticks and serve while warm.

Calories: 160
Fat: 2.5g
Sodium: 65mg
Carbs: 39.5g
Sugar: 22g
Protein: 4.5g

Grain and Fruit Cereal

Cynthia Haller, New Holland, PA

Makes 4–5 servings
Prep Time: 5 minutes ⚜ *Cooking Time: 3 hours* ⚜ *Ideal slow-cooker size: 4-qt.*

⅓ cup uncooked quinoa

⅓ cup uncooked millet

⅓ cup uncooked brown rice

4 cups water

¼ tsp. salt

½ cup raisins or dried cranberries

¼ cup chopped nuts, *optional*

1 tsp. vanilla extract, *optional*

½ tsp. ground cinnamon, *optional*

1 Tbsp. maple syrup, *optional*

1. Wash the quinoa, millet, and brown rice and rinse well.

2. Place the grains, water, and salt in a slow cooker. Cook on Low until most of the water has been absorbed, about 3 hours.

3. Add dried fruit and any optional ingredients, and cook for 30 minutes more. If the mixture is too thick, add a little more water.

4. Serve hot or cold.

Serving suggestion:

Add a little nondairy milk to each bowl of cereal before serving

Calories: 220
Fat: 2g
Sodium: 150mg
Carbs: 47g
Sugar: 11g
Protein: 5.5g

Breakfast Hominy

Bonnie Goering, Bridgewater, VA

Makes 5 servings
Prep Time: 5 minutes ⚜ *Cooking Time: 8 hours* ⚜ *Ideal slow-cooker size: 2-qt.*

1 cup dry cracked hominy
1 tsp. sea salt
black pepper, *optional*
3 cups water
2 Tbsp. butter

1. Stir all ingredients together in a greased slow cooker.

2. Cover and cook on Low 8 hours, or overnight.

3. Serve warm for breakfast.

Variation:

You can make cheesy hominy by decreasing the salt to ¾ tsp. and adding 1 cup grated cheese (we like American cheese best) to Step 1.

Cal: 140
Fat: 5g
Sodium: 450mg
Carbs: 24g
Sugar: 0g
Protein: 3g

Apple Breakfast Cobbler

Anona M. Teel, Bangor, PA

Makes 8 servings
Prep Time: 25 minutes ⚓ Cooking Time: 2–9 hours ⚓ Ideal slow-cooker size: 4- or 5-qt.

8 medium apples, cored, peeled, sliced

2 Tbsp. maple syrup

dash of cinnamon

juice of 1 lemon

2 Tbsp. coconut oil, melted

2 cups homemade gluten-free granola

1. Combine ingredients in the slow cooker.

2. Cover. Cook on Low 7–9 hours (while you sleep!), or on High 2–3 hours (after you're up in the morning).

TIP
If you don't have homemade granola, be sure to buy one with the least amount of sugar added to it.

Calories: 210
Fat: 18.5g
Sodium: 20mg
Carbs: 61g
Sugar: 34g
Protein: 9.5g

Breakfast Apples

Joyce Bowman, Lady Lake, FL
Jeanette Oberholtzer, Manheim, PA

Makes 4 servings
Prep Time: 10–15 minutes ⚭ Cooking Time: 2–8 hours ⚭ Ideal slow-cooker size: 3-qt.

4 medium-sized apples, peeled and sliced

¼ cup honey

1 tsp. cinnamon

2 Tbsp. melted coconut oil

2 cups dry gluten-free granola cereal

1. Place apples in your slow cooker.

2. Combine remaining ingredients. Sprinkle the mixture evenly over the apples.

3. Cover and cook on Low 6–8 hours, or overnight, or on High 2–3 hours.

4. Serve as a side dish to bacon and bagels, or use as a topping for waffles, French toast, pancakes, or cooked oatmeal.

TIP
Check the granola carefully. Many granolas have a lot of extra sugar added to them.

Cal: 520
Fat: 22g
Sodium: 20mg
Carbs: 73g
Sugar: 45g
Protein: 10g

Slow-cooker Yogurt

Becky Fixel, Grosse Pointe Farms, MI

Makes 12–14 servings

Prep Time: 2 minutes ⚬ *Cooking Time: 12–14 hours* ⚬ *Ideal slow-cooker size: 6-qt.*

I gallon whole milk

5.3 oz. Greek yogurt with cultures

1. Empty the gallon of whole milk into your slow cooker and put it on High heat for 2–4 hours. Length of time depends on your model, but the milk needs to heat to just below boiling point, about 180–200°F.

2. Turn off your slow cooker and let your milk cool down to 110–115°F. Again, this will take 2–4 hours. Set your starter Greek yogurt out so it can reach room temperature during this step.

3. In a small bowl, add about 1 cup of the warm milk and the Greek yogurt and mix together. Pour the mixture into the milk in the slow cooker and mix it in by stirring back and forth. Replace the lid of your slow cooker and wrap the whole thing in a towel. Let sit for 12–14 hours.

4. After 12 hours check on your glorious yogurt!

5. Line a colander with cheesecloth and place in bowl. Scoop your yogurt inside and let it sit for at least 4 hours. This will help separate the extra whey from the yogurt and thicken your final yogurt.

TIP

"My yogurt didn't all fit in one colander, but thankfully I had a second one to use. You can wait until the yogurt sinks down and there is more space in the colander if you only have one. Spoon finished yogurt into jars or containers and place in the fridge. After your yogurt is done, you're going to have leftover whey. Put it in a jar and pop it in the fridge. Use it to replace stock in recipes, water your plants, or to make cheese. It's amazing what you can do with it!"
—Becky Fixel

Calories: 190

Fat: 10g

Sodium: 130mg

Carbs: 14.5g

Sugar: 15.5g

Protein: 10g

Appetizers and Snacks

Artichokes

Gertrude Dutcher, Hartville, OH

Makes 4–6 servings
Prep Time: 15 minutes ⚜ Cooking Time: 6–8 hours ⚜ Ideal slow-cooker size: 4-qt.

4–6 artichokes

1 tsp. salt

1 cup lemon juice, *divided*

2 cups hot water

½ cup melted butter

1. Wash and trim artichokes. Cut off about 1″ from top. If you wish, trim tips of leaves. Stand chokes upright in the slow cooker.

2. Sprinkle each choke with ¼ tsp. salt and 2 Tbsp. lemon juice.

3. Pour 2 cups hot water around the base of the artichokes.

4. Cover and cook on Low 6–8 hours.

5. Serve with melted butter and lemon juice for dipping.

Cal: 210
Fat: 17g
Sodium: 310mg
Carbs: 16g
Sugar: 2g
Protein: 4g

Slow-cooked Salsa

Andy Wagner, Quarryville, PA

Makes 2 cups

Prep Time: 15 minutes   ☘   Cooking Time: 1½–3 hours   ☘   Standing Time: 2 hours   ☘   Ideal slow-cooker size: 3-qt.

10 plum tomatoes

2 garlic cloves

1 small onion, cut into wedges

1–2 jalapeños

½ cup chopped fresh cilantro

½ tsp. sea salt, *optional*

1. Core tomatoes. Cut a small slit in two tomatoes. Insert a garlic clove into each slit.

2. Place all tomatoes and onions in a 3-qt. slow cooker.

3. Cut stems off jalapeños. (Remove seeds if you want a milder salsa.) Place jalapeños in the slow cooker.

4. Cover and cook on High for 2½–3 hours or until vegetables are softened. Some may brown slightly. Cool at least 2 hours with the lid off.

5. In a blender, combine the tomato mixture, cilantro, and salt if you wish. Cover and process until blended.

6. Refrigerate leftovers.

Serving suggestion:

Garnish with cilantro and jalapeño.

TIP

Wear disposable gloves when cutting hot peppers; the oils can burn your skin. Avoid touching your face when you've been working with hot peppers.

Calories: 60

Fat: 0g

Sodium: 10mg

Carbs: 15g

Sugar: 13.5g

Protein: .5g

Mexican Dip

Marla Folkerts, Holland, OH

Makes 15 servings

Prep Time: 15–20 minutes ♣ Cooking Time: 2–3 hours ♣ Ideal slow-cooker size: 3-qt.

1 lb. low-fat ground beef or turkey

8-oz. pkg. low-fat Mexican cheese, grated

16-oz. jar gluten-free mild, thick, and chunky picante salsa, or thick and chunky salsa

6-oz. can refried beans

1. Brown meat in nonstick skillet.

2. Place meat and remaining ingredients into your crock and stir.

3. Cover and cook on Low for 3 hours, or until all ingredients are heated through and melted.

Serving suggestion:

Garnish with jalapeño.

Calories: 89
Fat: 4g
Sodium: 400mg
Carbs: 5g
Sugar: 2g
Protein: 9g

Prairie Fire Dip

Cheri Jantzen, Houston, TX

Makes 1¼ cups, or 10 servings
Prep Time: 5–10 minutes & Cooking Time: 1–3 hours & Ideal slow-cooker size: 2-qt.

1 cup gluten-free vegetarian refried fat-free beans (half a 15-oz. can)

½ cup shredded fat-free Monterey Jack cheese

¼ cup water

1 Tbsp. minced onion

1 clove garlic, minced

2 tsp. chili powder

hot sauce as desired

1. Combine all ingredients in the slow cooker.

2. Cover. Cook on High 1 hour, or on Low 2–3 hours. Serve with baked tortilla chips.

Serving suggestion:

Garnish with hot sauce and diced avocado.

Calories: 34
Fat: 1g
Sodium: 140mg
Carbs: 5g
Sugar: 0g
Protein: 3g

Slim Dunk

Vera Smucker, Goshen, IN

Makes 3 cups, or 12 servings
Prep Time: 20 minutes   ♣   Cooking Time: 1 hour   ♣   Ideal slow-cooker size: 1½-qt.

2 cups fat-free sour cream

¼ cup fat-free Miracle Whip salad dressing

10 oz. frozen chopped spinach, thawed and squeezed dry

1.8-oz. envelope dry leek soup mix

¼ cup minced red bell pepper

1. Combine all ingredients in the slow cooker. Mix well.

2. Cover and cook on High for 1 hour.

Serving Suggestion:

Serve with baked tortilla chips.

Cal: 70
Fat: 0g
Sodium: 760mg
Carbs: 15g
Sugar: 5g
Protein: 2g

French Onion Dip

Hope Comerford, Clinton Township, MI

Makes 6 servings
Prep Time: 10 minutes & Cooking Time: 8 hours & Ideal slow-cooker size: 2-qt.

2 large sweet yellow onions, finely chopped

4 Tbsp. olive oil

1½ cups plain nonfat Greek yogurt

2 cloves garlic, minced

2 tsp. Worcestershire sauce

¼ tsp. salt

¼ tsp. pepper

Pinch of cayenne

1. Place onions and olive oil in the crock and stir so onions are coated in the olive oil.

2. Cover and cook on Low for 8 hours, or until the onions are a deep caramel brown color.

3. Strain the onions.

4. In a bowl, combine yogurt, garlic, Worcestershire sauce, salt, pepper, cayenne, and onions.

Cal: 130
Fat: 9g
Sodium: 90mg
Carbs: 6g
Sugar: 3g
Protein: 6g

Seafood Dip

Joan Rosenberger, Stephens City, VA

Makes 24 servings of 2 Tbsp. each
Prep Time: 5–10 minutes ❧ *Cooking Time: 3 hours* ❧ *Ideal slow-cooker size: 3½-qt.*

10-oz. pkg. fat-free cream cheese
8-oz. pkg. imitation crab strands
2 Tbsp. finely chopped onion
4–5 drops hot sauce
¼ cup finely chopped walnuts
1 tsp. paprika

1. Blend all ingredients except nuts and paprika until well mixed.

2. Spread in the slow cooker. Sprinkle with nuts and paprika.

3. Cook on Low 3 hours.

Serving suggestion:

Garnish with paprika or cayenne pepper and parsley or cilantro.

Calories: 30
Fat: 1g
Sodium: 130mg
Carbs: 2.5g
Sugar: 1.5g
Protein: 3g

Gluten-Free Chex Mix

Hope Comerford, Clinton Township, MI

Makes 12 servings

Prep Time: 8 minutes ⚜ Cooking Time: 3 hours ⚜ Cooling Time: 1 hour ⚜ Ideal slow-cooker size: 6- or 7-qt.

4½ cups gluten-free Rice Chex

4½ cups gluten-free Cheerios

1 cup unsalted peanuts

⅓ cup coconut oil, melted

4 tsp. gluten-free Worcestershire sauce

1 tsp. sea salt

1 tsp. garlic powder

1 tsp. onion powder

1. Spray the crock with nonstick spray.

2. Place the Rice Chex, Cheerios, and peanuts in the crock.

3. In a small bowl, whisk together the coconut oil, Worcestershire sauce, sea salt, garlic powder, and onion powder. Pour this over the cereal in the crock and gently mix it with a rubber spatula until all cereal and peanuts are evenly coated.

4. Place a paper towel or thin dishcloth under the lid and cook on Low for 3 hours, stirring once at the end of the first hour, once at the end of the second hour, and twice the last hour.

5. Spread the mixture onto parchment paper-lined baking sheets and let them cool for 1 hour.

6. Serve or keep in a sealed container at room temperature for up to 3 weeks.

Calories: 210
Fat: 13g
Sodium: 350mg
Carbs: 21g
Sugar: 3g
Protein: 5g

Southern Boiled Peanuts

Mary June Hershberger, Lynchburg, VA

Makes 32 servings
Prep Time: 5 minutes & Cooking Time: 7–8 hours
Standing Time: 8 hours or overnight & Ideal slow-cooker size: 5-qt.

2 lbs. raw peanuts in the shell

7 Tbsp. salt

water to cover peanuts

1. Wash unshelled peanuts in water until the water is clear.

2. In your slow-cooker crock, soak peanuts overnight in water to cover, adding 7 Tbsp. salt.

3. In the morning, turn cooker to Low and cook for 7–10 hours until peanuts are desired tenderness. Boiled peanuts should be tender, not crunchy hard, and the shells will be quite soft.

4. Drain peanuts and allow to cool 10 minutes before serving. Peel shells off peanuts and eat.

5. Store leftover boiled peanuts in refrigerator, or freeze. Reheat before eating.

Calories: 170
Fat: 13g
Sodium: 540mg
Carbs: 7g
Sugar: 0g
Protein: 7g

Rhonda's Apple Butter

Rhonda Burgoon, Collingswood, NJ

Makes 24 servings (2 Tbsp. each)
Prep Time: 20 minutes ⚮ Cooking Time: 12–14 hours ⚮ Ideal slow-cooker size: 3-qt.

4 lbs. apples
2 tsp. cinnamon
½ tsp. ground cloves

1. Peel, core, and slice apples. Place in the slow cooker.

2. Cover. Cook on High 2–3 hours. Reduce to low and cook 8 hours. Apples should be a rich brown and be cooked down by half.

3. Stir in spices. Cook on High 2–3 hours with lid off. Stir until smooth.

4. Pour into freezer containers and freeze, or pour into sterilized jars and seal.

Calories: 40
Fat: 0g
Sodium: 0mg
Carbs: 10.5g
Sugar: 8g
Protein: 0g

Pear Honey Butter

Becky Fixel, Grosse Pointe Farms, MI

Makes 45–50 servings
Prep Time: 30 ⚶ Cooking Time: 10 hours ⚶ Ideal slow-cooker size: 6½- or 7-qt.

10 lbs. ripened pears, peeled, cored, sliced

1 cup water

1 cup honey

1. Place pear slices inside your slow cooker.

2. Add in the water and honey.

3. Cover and cook on Low for 10 hours. You can stir if you want to, but it's not necessary. When your pears are done, they will have darkened in color, but won't dry out through cooking.

4. Either use your blender and puree the softened pears in batches until done or use an immersion blender to make a smooth consistency.

Serving suggestion:

Serve on whole-grain bread with cream cheese and top with cinnamon.

TIP
Freeze or can the extras in a water bath for 20 minutes.

Calories: 80
Fat: 0g
Sodium: 0mg
Carbs: 20g
Sugar: 15g
Protein: .5g

Soups, Stews, and Chilies

Beef Barley Soup

Stacie Skelly, Millersville, PA

Makes 8–10 servings
Prep Time: 15 minutes & Cooking Time: 9¼–11½ hours & Ideal slow-cooker size: 6-qt.

3–4 lb. chuck roast

2 cups carrots, chopped

6 cups low-sodium vegetable
or tomato juice, *divided*

2 cups quick-cook barley
water, to desired consistency

salt and pepper to taste, *optional*

1. Place roast, carrots, and 4 cups juice in the slow cooker.

2. Cover and cook on Low 8–10 hours.

3. Remove roast. Place on platter and cover with foil to keep warm.

4. Meanwhile, add barley to the slow cooker. Stir well. Turn heat to High and cook 45 minutes to 1 hour, until barley is tender.

5. While barley is cooking, cut meat into bite-sized pieces.

6. When barley is tender, return chopped beef to the slow cooker. Add 2 cups juice, water if you wish, and salt and pepper, if you want. Cook for 30 minutes on High, or until soup is heated through.

Cal: 370
Fat: 10g
Sodium: 340mg
Carbs: 34g
Sugar: 4g
Protein: 36g

Easy Slow-cooker Vegetable Soup

Beth Peachey, Belleville, PA

Makes 8–10 servings

Prep Time: 10 minutes ♣ *Cooking Time: 6 hours* ♣ *Ideal slow-cooker size: 3-qt.*

1 cup carrots, chopped or sliced

1 cup green beans, fresh, frozen, or canned

1 cup corn, fresh, frozen or canned, and drained

1 qt. low-sodium canned tomatoes

1 cup cooked beef, cut in bite-sized pieces

1. Combine all ingredients in the slow cooker.

2. Cover and cook on Low 6–8 hours, or until vegetables are tender.

TIP
If you don't have cooked beef, cut raw beef into small pieces and cook for 8 hours.

Cal: 320

Fat: 18g

Sodium: 95mg

Carbs: 16g

Sugar: 4g

Protein: 24g

Beef Vegetable Soup

Margaret Moffitt, Bartlett, TN

Makes 12 servings
Prep Time: 15 minutes ❧ Cooking Time: 6–8 hours ❧ Ideal slow-cooker size: 4-qt.

1 lb. chunks of stewing beef

28-oz. can low-sodium stewed tomatoes, undrained

1 tomato can of water

16-oz. pkg. of your favorite frozen vegetable

half a 10-oz. pkg. frozen chopped onions

1 ½ tsp. salt

¼–½ tsp. pepper

2 Tbsp. chopped fresh parsley, *optional*

1. Combine all ingredients in the slow cooker.
2. Cover and cook on High 6–8 hours.

Cal: 110
Fat: 2.5g
Sodium: 340mg
Carbs: 12g
Sugar: 3g
Protein: 10g

Holiday Soup

Ruth Retter, Manheim, PA

Makes 12–16 servings

Prep Time: 10 minutes to precook the beans ❧ Cooking Time: 6½–9 hours ❧ Ideal slow-cooker size: 4-qt.

1 lb. holiday soup mix of dried beans, or your choice of 1 lb. of mixed dried beans

9 cups water

6 cups water

1 large onion, chopped

14-oz. can low-sodium stewed or whole tomatoes

juice of one lemon

2 ham hocks

1. Place dried beans in large stockpot and cover with 9 cups of water. Cover and bring to a boil on your stovetop. Continue boiling for 10 minutes.

2. Remove beans from heat, keeping covered. Allow to stand for 1 hour.

3. Return covered pot of beans to the stove and bring to a boil. Then turn to simmer and continue cooking, covered, for 2½–3 hours, or until beans are soft. Drain.

4. Place drained beans in the slow cooker. Add 6 cups water, chopped onion, tomatoes, lemon juice, and 2 ham hocks. Mix together well.

5. Cover and cook on High 3 hours, or on Low 5 hours.

6. Remove ham from bone. Cut meat into small pieces and stir into soup before serving.

Variations:

1. Add 1 tsp. chili powder to Step 4.

  —Ruth Ann Hoover, New Holland, PA

2. Add 1 cup carrots, 1 bay leaf, and salt and pepper to taste, to Step 4.

  —Deb Herr, Mountaintop, PA

Cal: 120
Fat: 1.5g
Sodium: 170mg
Carbs: 20g
Sugar: 2g
Protein: 8g

Beans with Tomatoes and Ham

Kristin Tice, Shipshewana, IN

Makes 10 servings

Prep Time: 10–20 minutes ⚓ *Cooking Time: 7½–9½ hours* ⚓ *Ideal slow-cooker size: 5- to 6-qt.*

3 cups dried beans (great northern, navy, black, or pinto, or a combination of any of them)

12 cups water

4 cups fresh tomatoes, chopped, or 28-oz. can low-sodium stewed or diced tomatoes, drained

½ cup chopped onion

1 tsp. salt

4 cups water

2 cups ham

1. Place beans and 12 cups water in a large stockpot. Cover and bring to a boil.

2. Uncover and boil for 2 minutes.

3. Cover, remove from heat, and set aside for 1 hour. Drain beans.

4. Place beans in the slow cooker. Add tomatoes, onion, salt, and 4 cups water.

5. Cover and cook on High 6–8 hours, or until beans are tender.

6. After beans are tender, stir in ham and cook an additional 30 minutes on Low.

Cal: 240
Fat: 2.5g
Sodium: 230mg
Carbs: 39g
Sugar: 3g
Protein: 18g

Old-Fashioned Bean Soup

Shirley Sears, Sarasota, FL

Makes 8–10 servings
Prep Time: 10 minutes ❧ Cooking Time: 13–20 hours ❧ Ideal slow-cooker size: 4- to 5-qt.

1 lb. dried navy beans, soaked overnight
16 cups water, *divided*
1 lb. meaty ham bones, or ham pieces
1 tsp. salt
½ tsp. pepper
½ cup chopped celery leaves
1 medium onion, chopped
1 bay leaf, *optional*

1. Place dried beans and 8 cups water in a large stockpot. Cover and allow to soak for 8 hours or overnight. Drain.

2. Place soaked beans and 8 cups fresh water in your slow cooker.

3. Add all remaining ingredients.

4. Cover and cook on Low 10–12 hours, or on High 5–6 hours, or until the meat is falling off the bone and the beans are tender but not mushy.

Cal: 220
Fat: 3g
Sodium: 570mg
Carbs: 30g
Sugar: 2g
Protein: 20g

Split Pea Soup with Ham

Elena Yoder, Carlsbad, NM

Makes 8 servings
Prep Time: 15 minutes   ♣   Cooking Time: 4 hours   ♣   Ideal slow-cooker size: 4-qt.

2½ qts. water
1 ham hock or pieces of cut-up ham
2½ cups split peas, dried
1 medium onion, chopped
3 medium carrots, cut in small pieces
salt and pepper to taste

1. Bring water to a boil in a saucepan on your stovetop.

2. Place all other ingredients into the slow cooker. Add water and stir together well.

3. Cover and cook on High for 4 hours, or until vegetables are tender.

4. If you've cooked a ham hock, remove it from the soup and debone the meat. Stir cut-up chunks of meat back into the soup before serving.

Cal: 230
Fat: 1.5g
Sodium: 140mg
Carbs: 39g
Sugar: 6g
Protein: 17g

Navy Bean and Ham Soup

Jennifer Freed, Rockingham, VA

Makes 6 servings

Prep Time: overnight, or approximately 8 hours   ❧   Cooking Time: 8–10 hours   ❧   Ideal slow-cooker size: 6½- or 7-qt.

6 cups water

5 cups dried navy beans, soaked overnight, drained, and rinsed

1 pound ham, cubed

15-oz. can corn, drained

4-oz. can mild diced green chiles, drained

1 onion, diced, *optional*

salt and pepper to taste

1. Place all ingredients in the slow cooker.

2. Cover and cook on Low 8–10 hours, or until beans are tender.

Calories: 420
Fat: 5g
Sodium: 1200mg
Carbs: 103g
Sugar: 7g
Protein: 44g

Easy Beef Stew

Judi Manos, West Islip, NY

Makes 4–6 servings
Prep Time: 20 minutes ⚜ Cooking Time: 7½–8½ hours ⚜ Ideal slow-cooker size: 4-qt.

4 medium-sized red potatoes

1½ lbs. beef stew meat

⅓ cup gluten-free flour

14-oz. can low-sodium diced tomatoes, undrained

2 cups water

3 cups frozen stir-fry bell peppers and onions

1. Cut potatoes into quarters. Place on bottom of slow cooker.

2. In a mixing bowl, toss beef with flour to coat. Add to the slow cooker.

3. Pour in undrained tomatoes and water.

4. Cover and cook on Low 7–8 hours, or until beef and potatoes are tender but not overcooked.

5. Gently fold stir-fry vegetables into stew. Cover and cook on Low 30-40 minutes, or until vegetables are hot and tender.

Variations:

1. Add 2–3 cups sliced carrots just after the potatoes in Step 1.

2. Add 2 tsp. salt and ¾ tsp. pepper to the flour in Step 2, before tossing with the beef.

Cal: 320
Fat: 18g
Sodium: 95mg
Carbs:16g
Sugar: 4g
Protein: 24g

Succulent Beef Stew

Linda Thomas, Sayner, WI

Makes 6 servings

Prep Time: 30 minutes ⚜ *Cooking Time: 8 hours* ⚜ *Ideal slow-cooker size: 3-qt.*

1–1½ lbs. stew meat

1 medium to large onion, chopped

salt and pepper, *optional*

1¾ cups low-sodium, gluten-free beef broth

1 broth can of water

5 shakes Worcestershire sauce, *optional*

2 bay leaves, *optional*

½ lb. baby carrots

5 medium white potatoes, peeled or unpeeled, cut into ½" chunks

1. In a nonstick skillet, brown stew meat and chopped onion. Sprinkle with salt and pepper if you wish. Transfer mixture to the slow cooker.

2. Add broth and water, and Worcestershire sauce and bay leaves if you choose to. Stir together well.

3. Cover and cook on Low 4 hours.

4. Layer in vegetables. Push down into liquid as much as you can. Cover and continue cooking on Low for 4 more hours.

5. If the stew seems to get dry, add ½ cup water.

Cal: 310

Fat: 18g

Sodium: 400mg

Carbs: 15g

Sugar: 4g

Protein: 24g

Roast Beef Stew

Thelma Good, Harrisonburg, VA

Makes 8 servings
Prep Time: 10–15 minutes   Cooking Time: 8–11 hours   Ideal slow-cooker size: 6-qt.

2–3-lb. roast
5–6 potatoes, quartered
4–5 carrots, sliced
2 small onions, sliced
half a head of cabbage, sliced

1. Place roast in crock.

2. Cover and cook on Low for 6–8 hours.

3. Place the potatoes, carrots, and onions around and over the roast. Fill slow cooker ½–¾ full with water, depending upon how soupy you like your stew.

4. Cover and cook on High 2–3 hours.

5. Lift the lid and put in the cabbage, pushing it down into the broth. Continue cooking on High 1 more hour, or until veggies are done to your liking. The stew should be ready at lunchtime—or dinnertime.

Variations:

1. Sprinkle the roast, top and bottom, with salt and pepper before placing it in the cooker in Step 1. Also, sprinkle the vegetables with salt after you've put them in the cooker in Step 3.

2. Increase the amount of potatoes, carrots, onions, and cabbage to your liking. You may need to increase the cooking time in Steps 4 and 5 to make sure that they get as tender as you like.

Cal: 300
Fat: 3g
Sodium: 120mg
Carbs: 17g
Sugar: 5g
Protein: 40g

Mediterranean Beef Stew

Sandy Osborn, Iowa City, IA

Makes 4 servings
Prep Time: 5–10 minutes ⚓ *Cooking Time: 3–8 hours* ⚓ *Ideal slow-cooker size: 3½-qt.*

2 medium-sized zucchini, cut into bite-sized pieces

¾ pound beef stew meat, cut into ½" pieces

2 14½-oz. cans Italian-style diced tomatoes, undrained

½ tsp. pepper, *optional*

2" stick cinnamon, or ¼ tsp. ground cinnamon

1. Place zucchini in the bottom of your slow cooker.

2. Add beef and remaining ingredients in the order they are listed.

3. Cover and cook on High 3–5 hours, or until the meat is tender but not overcooked. You can also cook the stew on High 1 hour, then on Low for 7 hours, or until meat is tender but not overdone. Remove cinnamon stick before serving.

Cal: 170
Fat: 5g
Sodium: 85mg
Carbs: 12g
Sugar: 8g
Protein: 21g

Hearty Lentil and Sausage Stew

Cindy Krestynick, Glen Lyon, PA

Makes 6 servings
Prep Time: 5–10 minutes ⚬ Cooking Time: 4–6 hours ⚬ Ideal slow-cooker size: 6-qt.

2 cups dry lentils,
picked over and rinsed

14½-oz. can low-sodium diced
tomatoes

8 cups gluten-free low-sodium
chicken broth, or water

1 Tbsp. salt

½–1 lb. pork or beef sausage,
cut into 2" pieces

1. Place lentils, tomatoes, chicken broth, and salt in the slow cooker. Stir to combine. Place sausage pieces on top.

2. Cover and cook on Low 4–6 hours, or until lentils are tender but not dry or mushy.

Cal: 560
Fat: 25g
Sodium: 1780mg
Carbs: 56g
Sugar: 10g
Protein: 34g

Pork Potato Soup

Kristin Tice, Shipshewana, IN

Makes 4 servings
Prep Time: 20 minutes ❧ *Cooking Time: 4 hours* ❧ *Ideal slow-cooker size: 3-qt.*

1 lb. ground pork

½ cup chopped onion

1 sweet potato, peeled and cubed, approximately 3 cups

2 gluten-free, low-sodium beef bouillon cubes

½ tsp. dried rosemary

3 cups water

1. Place meat and onion in nonstick skillet. Brown on stovetop.

2. Place drained meat, along with onion, into the slow cooker. Add remaining ingredients.

3. Cover and cook on Low for 4 hours.

Serving Suggestion: Add a bit of hot sauce to make the soup spicy, or serve on the side to accommodate those who don't like hot food.

Cal: 380
Fat: 20g
Sodium: 310mg
Carbs: 27g
Sugar: 7g
Protein: 25g

Chicken Rice Soup

Norma Grieser, Clarksville, MI

Makes 8 servings
Prep Time: 30 minutes ❧ Cooking Time: 4–8 hours ❧ Ideal slow-cooker size: 4- to 6-qt.

4 cups gluten-free low-sodium chicken broth

4 cups cut-up chicken, cooked

1⅓ cups cut-up celery

1⅓ cups diced carrots

1 qt. water

1 cup uncooked long-grain rice

1. Put all ingredients in the slow cooker.

2. Cover and cook on Low 4–8 hours, or until vegetables are cooked to your liking.

Cal: 250
Fat: 4g
Sodium: 260mg
Carbs: 25g
Sugar: 3g
Protein: 27g

Split Pea with Chicken Soup

Mary E. Wheatley, Mashpee, MA

Makes 6–8 servings
Prep Time: 20 minutes   ⚬   Cooking Time: 4–10 hours   ⚬   Ideal slow-cooker size: 5-qt.

16-oz. pkg. dried split peas

¾ cup finely diced carrots

3 cups cubed raw potatoes

8 cups gluten-free low-sodium chicken broth

1 cup diced cooked chicken

1. Combine peas, carrots, potatoes, and chicken broth in the slow cooker.

2. Cook on High 4–5 hours, or on Low 8–10 hours, or until all vegetables are tender. Stir after the soup begins to slowly boil.

3. Ten minutes before serving, stir in cooked chicken.

Cal: 380
Fat: 5g
Sodium: 390mg
Carbs: 57g
Sugar: 10g
Protein: 27g

Chipotle Navy Bean Soup

Rebecca Weybright, Manheim, PA

Makes 6 servings
Prep Time: 10 minutes & Cooking Time: 8 hours & Standing Time: 12 hours & Ideal slow-cooker size: 5-qt.

1½ cups dried navy beans, soaked overnight

1 onion, chopped

1 dried chipotle chile, soaked 10–15 minutes in cold water

4 cups water

1–2 tsp. salt

2 cups canned reduced-sodium tomatoes with juice

1. Drain soaked beans.

2. Add to the slow cooker with onion, chile, and 4 cups water.

3. Cover and cook on Low for 8 hours until beans are creamy.

4. Add salt and tomatoes.

5. Use an immersion blender to puree soup.

Calories: 200
Fat: 1g
Sodium: 600mg
Carbs: 36g
Sugar: 5g
Protein: 12.5g

Slow-cooker Tomato Soup

Becky Fixel, Grosse Pointe Farms, MI

Makes 8 servings
Prep Time: 15 minutes ⚓ *Cooking Time: 6 hours* ⚓ *Ideal slow-cooker size: 6-qt.*

6–8 cups chopped fresh tomatoes

1 medium onion, chopped

2 tsp. minced garlic

1 tsp. basil

½ tsp. pepper

½ tsp. sea salt

½ tsp. red pepper flakes

2 Tbsp. Massel chicken bouillon

1 cup water

¾ cup fat-free half-and-half

1. Combine tomatoes, onion, spices, chicken bouillon, and 1 cup of water in your slow cooker.

2. Cover and cook on Low for 6 hours.

3. Add in ¾ cup fat-free half-and-half and combine all ingredients with an immersion blender. Serve hot.

Calories: 70
Fat: 0g
Sodium: 470mg
Carbs: 11g
Sugar: 6g
Protein: 1g

Italian Bean Soup

Eylene Egan, Babylon, NY

Makes 8 servings
Prep Time: 10 minutes & Cooking Time: 8–10 hours & Ideal slow-cooker size: 4-qt.

1 lb. dried baby lima beans

9 cups water

2 8-oz. cans low-sodium tomato sauce

3–4 cloves garlic, minced

6 cups water

salt and pepper to taste

1. Place dried beans in large stockpot. Cover with 9 cups water. Cover pot and bring to a boil.

2. Boil for 10 minutes. Remove from heat and allow beans to stand for 1 hour, covered.

3. Return to the stovetop, keep covered, and bring to a boil. Reduce heat to a simmer, and continue cooking for 2½-3 hours, or until beans are tender. Drain.

4. Place drained, cooked beans in the slow cooker. Add remaining ingredients and stir together well.

5. Cover and cook on High 1 hour, and then cook on Low 4–5 hours.

Cal: 80
Fat: 0.5g
Sodium: 310mg
Carbs: 15g
Sugar: 3g
Protein: 5g

Potato Soup with Possibilities

Janie Steele, Moore, OK

Makes 6 servings

Prep Time: 20–30 minutes ⚭ Cooking Time: 5–6 hours ⚭ Ideal slow-cooker size: 4- to 6-qt.

6–8 cups homemade chicken broth (use vegetable broth to keep this vegetarian/vegan)

1 large onion, chopped

3 celery stalks, chopped, including leaves, if you like

6 large white potatoes, peeled, chopped, cubed, or sliced

salt and pepper to taste

reduced-fat shredded sharp cheddar cheese, *optional*

2–3 cups chopped clams, *optional*

10- or 16-oz. pkg. frozen corn, *optional*

1. Place all ingredients in the slow cooker.

2. Cover and cook on High 5 hours, or on Low 6 hours, or until vegetables are soft but not mushy.

TIP

If you don't have homemade chicken broth, use a low-sodium chicken stock.

Cal: 180
Fat: 4g
Sodium: 490mg
Carbs: 25g
Sugar: 7g
Protein: 10g

Butternut Squash Soup

Elaine Vigoda, Rochester, NY

Makes 4–6 servings
Prep Time: 5 minutes ☙ *Cooking Time: 4–8 hours* ☙ *Ideal slow-cooker size: 4- to 5-qt.*

5½ cups low-sodium, gluten-free chicken broth (use vegetable broth to keep this vegetarian/vegan)

1 medium-sized butternut squash, peeled and cubed

1 small onion, chopped

1 tsp. ground ginger

1 tsp. garlic, minced, *optional*

¼ tsp. nutmeg, *optional*

1. Place chicken broth and squash in the slow cooker. Add remaining ingredients.

2. Cover and cook on High 4 hours, or on Low 6–8 hours, or until squash is tender.

Cal: 120
Fat: 3g
Sodium: 320mg
Carbs: 18g
Sugar: 6g
Protein: 6g

Chili with Two Beans

Patricia Fleischer, Carlisle, PA

Makes 6–8 servings
Prep Time: 15 minutes ☙ *Cooking Time: 4½–5 hours* ☙ *Ideal slow-cooker size: 6-qt.*

1 lb. lean ground beef

6-oz. can low-sodium tomato paste

40½-oz. can low-sodium
kidney beans, undrained

2 15½-oz. cans low-sodium
pinto beans, undrained

2 Tbsp. chili powder

1. Brown beef in large nonstick skillet. Drain.

2. Combine all ingredients in the slow cooker.

3. Cover and cook on Low 4½–5 hours.

Cal: 340
Fat: 9g
Sodium: 460mg
Carbs: 43g
Sugar: 7g
Protein: 25g

Easy Spicy Chili

Becky Gehman, Bergton, VA

Makes 9–12 servings
Prep Time: 15 minutes ♣ Cooking Time: 4–10 hours ♣ Ideal slow-cooker size: 4- to 5-qt.

2 lbs. lean ground beef

3 15½-oz. cans low-sodium red kidney beans, drained

2–3 14½-oz. cans low-sodium diced tomatoes, undrained

2 onions, chopped

1 green pepper, chopped, *optional*

2–3 Tbsp. chili powder

1. Brown ground beef in a large nonstick skillet. Drain.

2. Place beef in the slow cooker. Add kidney beans, tomatoes, onions, and green pepper, if you wish, to the cooker. Fold together well.

3. Cover and cook on Low 8–10 hours or on High 4–6 hours.

4. Add chili powder 2 hours before the end of the cooking time.

TIPS

1. This can be successfully frozen and reheated later.

2. You may want to pass salt and pepper as you serve the chili.

3. You may add about 2 Tbsp. of flour along with the chili powder in Step 4 if you want to thicken the chili.

Cal: 250
Fat: 10g
Sodium: 210mg
Carbs: 20g
Sugar: 3g
Protein: 21g

Chunky Chili

Eleanor Larson, Glen Lyon, PA

Makes 4–5 servings
Prep Time: 10 minutes ⚬ *Cooking Time: 4–5 hours* ⚬ *Ideal slow-cooker size: 3-qt.*

1½ lbs. cubed beef stew meat, or venison

1 medium-sized onion, chopped

1 or 2 8-oz. cans low-sodium tomato sauce, depending upon how thick or thin you prefer chili to be

1½–3 tsp. chili powder, depending upon your taste preference

16-oz. can low-sodium kidney beans, drained

1. Place all ingredients in the slow cooker. Mix well.

2. Cover and cook on High 4–5 hours, or until the meat is tender but not overcooked.

Cal: 310
Fat: 8g
Sodium: 570mg
Carbs: 24g
Sugar: 3g
Protein: 38g

Beef and Beans

Margaret H. Moffitt, Bartlet, TN

Makes 4–6 servings
Prep Time: 20–25 minutes   ❧   Cooking Time: 4–6 hours   ❧   Ideal slow-cooker size: 3-qt.

1 ½ lbs. lean ground beef

15-oz. can tomato sauce with garlic and onion

2 15-oz. cans low-sodium kidney beans, undrained

salt and pepper to taste

1. Brown beef in a nonstick skillet, just until the pink is gone. Drain.

2. Place beef in bottom of slow cooker.

3. Add tomato sauce, beans, and salt and pepper.

4. Cover and cook on Low 4–6 hours.

Variations:

1. For a juicier dish to serve over rice, use two cans of tomato sauce.

2. For more texture, substitute petite-cut tomatoes with garlic and onion in place of the tomato sauce.

—Anita Wansley

Cal: 350
Fat: 15g
Sodium: 610mg
Carbs: 25g
Sugar: 6g
Protein: 30g

Main Dishes

BEEF

Pot Roast with Carrots and Potatoes

Loretta Hanson, Hendricks, MN

Makes 6 servings
Prep Time: 30 minutes ☙ Cooking Time: 4–12 hours ☙ Ideal slow-cooker size: 5- to 6-qt.

3–4 potatoes, pared and thinly sliced
3–4 carrots, pared and thinly sliced
1 onion, chopped, *optional*
salt and pepper to taste
3-lb. brisket, rump roast, or pot roast
1 cup low-sodium, gluten-free beef stock

1. Place vegetables in bottom of slow cooker.

2. Salt and pepper meat. Place meat in the slow cooker.

3. Pour beef stock around meat.

4. Cover and cook on Low 10–12 hours, or on High 4–5 hours.

Variation:

Add 2–3 Tbsp. Worcestershire sauce in Step 3, before adding the beef broth.

—Carol Eveleth, Wellman, IA

Cal: 420
Fat: 20g
Sodium: 280mg
Carbs: 11g
Sugar: 3g
Protein: 47g

Italian Roast with Potatoes

Ruthie Schiefer, Vassar, MI

Makes 8 servings
Prep Time: 30–35 minutes & Cooking Time: 6–7 hours & Ideal slow-cooker size: 5-qt.

6 medium-sized potatoes, peeled if you wish, and quartered

1 large onion, sliced

3–4-lb. boneless beef roast

26-oz. jar gluten-free tomato and basil pasta sauce, *divided*

½ cup water

3 low-sodium, gluten-free beef bouillon cubes

1. Place potatoes and onion in bottom of slow cooker.

2. Meanwhile, brown roast on top and bottom in nonstick skillet.

3. Place roast on top of vegetables. Pour any drippings from the skillet over the beef.

4. Mix 1 cup pasta sauce and ½ cup water together in a small bowl. Stir in bouillon cubes. Spoon mixture over meat.

5. Cover and cook on Low 6–7 hours, or until meat is tender but not dry.

6. Transfer roast and vegetables to serving platter. Cover with foil.

7. Take 1 cup cooking juices from the slow cooker and place in medium-sized saucepan. Stir in remaining pasta sauce. Heat.

8. Slice or cube beef. Pour sauce over the meat and vegetables or serve on the side.

Cal: 290
Fat: 9g
Sodium: 560mg
Carbs: 13g
Sugar: 5g
Protein: 40g

Uncle Tim's Pot Roast

Tim Smith, Rutledge, PA

Makes 4 servings
Prep Time: 30 minutes ♣ Cooking Time: 8 hours ♣ Ideal slow-cooker size: 5-qt.

4-lb. eye of round roast beef

2 Tbsp. crushed garlic

8 medium-sized red potatoes, halved or quartered

I lb. baby carrots, peeled

water

I green pepper, cut in half and deseeded

1. Place roast in center of slow cooker. Rub garlic into roast.

2. Add potatoes and carrots. Add water until carrots and potatoes are covered.

3. Cover and cook on Low for 8 hours.

4. One hour before serving, place pepper halves on top of meat (moving vegetables aside as much as possible), cut-side down. Cover and continue cooking.

Variation:

Sprinkle roast with salt and pepper in Step 1, and sprinkle potatoes and carrots with salt in Step 2.

Cal: 660
Fat: 12g
Sodium: 330mg
Carbs: 30g
Sugar: 7g
Protein: 110g

Italian Roast Beef

Dorothy VanDeest, Memphis, TN

Makes 6–8 servings
Prep Time: 15 minutes ♣ *Cooking Time: 10–12 hours* ♣ *Ideal slow-cooker size: 4- to 5-qt.*

2 onions, *divided*

2 cloves garlic

1 large rib of celery,
chopped fine, *optional*

3 slices bacon

4-lb. beef rump roast

1. Finely chop 1 onion, the garlic, celery, and bacon. Mix together.

2. Rub roast on all sides with minced mixture.

3. Slice remaining onion. Place in the slow cooker. Place roast on top of onion.

4. Sprinkle any remaining rub—or any that's fallen off the roast—over the meat.

5. Cover and cook on Low 10–12 hours.

Cal: 380
Fat: 18g
Sodium: 150mg
Carbs: 3g
Sugar: 1g
Protein: 51g

Peppercorn Beef Roast

Stacie Skelly, Millersville, PA

Makes 6–8 servings
Prep Time: 10–15 minutes ⚜ *Cooking Time: 8–10 hours* ⚜ *Ideal slow-cooker size: 4-qt.*

3–4-lb. chuck roast

½ cup gluten-free, reduced-sodium soy sauce or liquid aminos

1 tsp. garlic powder

1 bay leaf

3–4 peppercorns

2 cups water

1 tsp. thyme, *optional*

1. Place roast in the slow cooker.

2. In a mixing bowl, combine all other ingredients and pour over roast.

3. Cover and cook on Low 8–10 hours.

4. Remove meat to a platter and allow to rest before slicing or shredding.

TIP
To make gravy to go with the meat, whisk together ½ cup of gluten-free flour and ½ cup water, stir into meat juices in crock, turn cooker to High, and bring cooking juices to a boil until gravy is thickened.

Cal: 410
Fat: 25g
Sodium: 570mg
Carbs: 3g
Sugar: 1g
Protein: 44g

Beef Roast with Tomatoes, Onions, and Peppers

Donna Treloar, Hartford City, IN

Makes 10 servings
Prep Time: 15 minutes ❧ *Cooking Time: 8–10 hours* ❧ *Ideal slow-cooker size: 4-qt.*

4–5-lb. beef roast

2 14½-oz. cans Mexican-style stewed tomatoes

16-oz. jar gluten-free salsa, your choice of mild, medium, or hot

2 or 3 medium-sized onions, cut in chunks

1 or 2 green or red bell peppers, sliced

1. Brown the roast on top and bottom in a nonstick skillet and place in the slow cooker.

2. In a bowl, combine stewed tomatoes and salsa. Spoon over meat.

3. Cover and cook on Low 8–10 hours, or until the meat is tender but not dry.

4. Add onions halfway through cooking time in order to keep fairly crisp. Push down into the sauce.

5. One hour before serving, add pepper slices. Push down into the sauce.

6. Remove meat from cooker and allow to rest 10 minutes before slicing. Place slices on serving platter and top with vegetables and sauce.

TIP

Make Easy Beef Burritos with the leftovers. Shred any leftover beef with 2 forks. Heat on the stovetop with the peppers, onions, and ½ cup sauce. Add 1 Tbsp. chili powder, 2 tsp. cumin, and salt to taste. Heat through. Spoon onto warm flour tortillas. Serve with salsa, sour cream, and/or guacamole.

Cal: 340
Fat: 12g
Sodium: 770mg
Carbs: 17g
Sugar: 6g
Protein: 43g

Spicy Beef Roast

Karen Ceneviva, Seymour, CT

Makes 10 servings

Prep Time: 15–20 minutes ❧ *Cooking Time: 3–8 hours* ❧ *Ideal slow-cooker size: 4- or 5-qt.*

1–2 Tbsp. cracked black peppercorns

2 cloves garlic, minced

3-lb. eye of round roast, trimmed of fat

3 Tbsp. balsamic vinegar

¼ cup gluten-free reduced-sodium soy sauce or Bragg's liquid aminos

2 Tbsp. gluten-free Worcestershire sauce

2 tsp. dry mustard

1. Rub cracked pepper and garlic onto roast. Put roast in the slow cooker.

2. Make several shallow slits in top of meat.

3. In a small bowl, combine remaining ingredients. Spoon over meat.

4. Cover and cook on Low for 6–8 hours, or on High for 3–4 hours, just until meat is tender, but not dry.

Calories: 240

Fat: 6g

Sodium: 530mg

Carbs: 2g

Sugar: 1g

Protein: 41.5g

Green Chile Roast

Anna Kenagy, Carlsbad, NM

Makes 8–10 servings
Prep Time: 15 minutes ❧ Cooking Time: 8 hours ❧ Ideal slow-cooker size: 4-qt.

3–4-lb. beef roast

1 tsp. salt

3–4 green chiles or 4-oz. can green chiles, undrained

1 Tbsp. gluten-free Worcestershire sauce

½ tsp. black pepper

1. Place roast in the slow cooker.

2. Pour in water until roast is half covered.

3. Add remaining ingredients over top.

4. Cover. Cook on Low 8 hours.

5. Serve with mashed potatoes and green beans.

Cal: 190
Fat: 7g
Sodium: 230mg
Carbs: 1g
Sugar: 0g
Protein: 30g

Low-Fat Slow-cooker Roast

Charlotte Shaffer, East Earl, PA

Makes 10 servings

Prep Time: 15 minutes ❧ *Cooking Time: 3–8 hours* ❧ *Ideal slow-cooker size: 6-qt.*

3-lb. boneless beef roast

4 carrots, peeled and cut into 2-inch pieces

4 potatoes, cut into quarters

2 onions, quartered

1 cup gluten-free, low-sodium beef broth or stock

1 tsp. garlic powder

1 tsp. Mrs. Dash seasoning

½ tsp. salt

½ tsp. black pepper

1. Place roast in the slow cooker.

2. Add carrots around edges, pushing them down so they reach the bottom of the crock.

3. Add potatoes and onions.

4. Mix together broth and seasonings and pour over roast.

5. Cover and cook on Low for 6–8 hours or on High for 3–4 hours.

Calories: 340
Fat: 12g
Sodium: 275mg
Carbs: 20g
Sugar: 3g
Protein: 39g

Hungarian Beef with Paprika

Maureen Csikasz, Wakefield, MA

Makes 9 servings
Prep Time: 15 minutes & Cooking Time: 3–6 hours & Ideal slow-cooker size: oval 5- or 6-qt. oval

3-lb. boneless chuck roast
2–3 medium onions, coarsely chopped
5 Tbsp. sweet paprika
¾ tsp. salt
¼ tsp. black pepper
½ tsp. caraway seeds
1 clove garlic, chopped
½ green bell pepper, sliced
¼ cup water
½ cup nonfat plain Greek yogurt
fresh parsley

1. Grease interior of slow-cooker crock.

2. Place roast in crock.

3. In a good-sized bowl, mix all ingredients together, except nonfat plain Greek yogurt and parsley.

4. Spoon evenly over roast.

5. Cover. Cook on High 3–4 hours, or on Low 5–6 hours, or until instant-read meat thermometer registers 140–145°F when stuck in center of meat.

6. When finished cooking, use sturdy tongs or 2 metal spatulas to lift meat to cutting board. Cover with foil to keep warm. Let stand 10–15 minutes.

7. Cut into chunks or slices.

8. Just before serving, dollop with nonfat plain Greek yogurt. Garnish with fresh parsley.

Calories: 250
Fat: 10.5g
Sodium: 320mg
Carbs: 6.5g
Sugar: 2.5g
Protein: 34.5g

Sweet-and-Sour Roast

Rosalie D. Miller, Mifflintown, PA

Makes 5 servings
Prep Time: 5 minutes   ⚬   Cooking Time: 6–8 hours   ⚬   Ideal slow-cooker size: 2-qt.

2-lb. beef roast

½ cup apple cider vinegar

3 Tbsp. turbinado sugar

2 tsp. salt

1 Tbsp. gluten-free Worcestershire sauce

1 cup water

1. Place roast in your slow cooker.

2. In a small bowl, combine remaining ingredients. Pour over the roast.

3. Cover and cook on Low 6–8 hours, or until meat is tender but not dry.

Variation:

Place 5 medium-sized potatoes, cubed, in the bottom of the cooker. Add enough water to just cover the potatoes. Top with 1 qt. frozen green beans. Then add roast and continue with Step 2 above.

Cal: 260
Fat: 9g
Sodium: 560mg
Carbs: 4g
Sugar: 3g
Protein: 40g

Herby French Dip Sandwiches

Sara Wichert, Hillsboro, KS

Makes 6–8 servings

Prep Time: 5 minutes ⚜ *Cooking Time: 5–6 hours* ⚜ *Ideal slow-cooker size: 4-qt.*

3-lb. chuck roast

2 cups water

½ cup gluten-free, low-sodium soy sauce or liquid aminos

1 tsp. garlic powder

1 bay leaf

3–4 whole peppercorns

1 tsp. dried rosemary, *optional*

1 tsp. dried thyme, *optional*

1. Place roast in the slow cooker.

2. Combine remaining ingredients in a mixing bowl. Pour over meat.

3. Cover and cook on High 5–6 hours, or until meat is tender but not dry.

4. Remove meat from broth and shred with fork. Stir back into sauce.

5. Remove meat from the cooker by large forkfuls.

Serving Suggestion:

Serve on French Rolls or Gluten-Free Rolls.

Cal: 240
Fat: 10g
Sodium: 580mg
Carbs: 3g
Sugar: 1g
Protein: 36g

Slow-cooker Swiss Steak

Joyce Bowman, Lady Lake, FL

Makes 4 servings
Prep Time: 30 minutes   ♣   Cooking Time: 7 hours   ♣   Ideal slow-cooker size: 3-qt.

1-lb. round steak, ¾–1" thick, cubed

16-oz. can low-sodium stewed tomatoes

3 carrots, halved lengthwise

2 potatoes, quartered

1 medium-sized onion, quartered

garlic powder to taste, *optional*

1. Add all ingredients to your slow cooker in the order they are listed.

2. Cover and cook on Low for 7 hours, or until meat and vegetables are tender, but not overcooked or dry.

Cal: 260
Fat: 6g
Sodium: 610mg
Carbs: 24g
Sugar: 5g
Protein: 30g

New Mexico Steak

Mamie Christopherson, Rio Rancho, NM

Makes 4–6 servings
Prep Time: 10 minutes ⚘ *Cooking Time: 4 hours* ⚘ *Ideal slow-cooker size: 3-qt.*

I large onion, sliced

2-lb. round steak,
cut into serving-size pieces

salt and pepper to taste

1¾ cup gluten-free green chile salsa

1. Place onion slices in bottom of slow cooker.

2. Sprinkle steak with salt and pepper. Add steak pieces to cooker.

3. Spoon chile salsa over all, being careful not to wash off the seasonings.

4. Cover and cook on High 1 hour. Turn to Low and cook 3 hours, or until steak is tender but not overcooked.

Cal: 200
Fat: 4g
Sodium: 480mg
Carbs: 5g
Sugar: 2g
Protein: 37g

Pepper Steak

Darlene G. Martin Richfield, PA

Makes 4 servings
Prep Time: 15–20 minutes ♣ Cooking Time: 5–6 hours ♣ Ideal slow-cooker size: 3½- to 4-qt.

1-lb. round steak, cut ¾–1" thick

14½-oz. can Italian-style stewed tomatoes, undrained

1 tsp. gluten-free Worcestershire sauce

2 yellow, 2 red, and 2 green bell peppers, sliced in strips

large onion, sliced

1. Cut meat into 4 serving-size pieces. In a large nonstick skillet, brown meat on both sides. Transfer meat to a 3½- or 4-qt. slow cooker.

2. In medium bowl, stir together undrained tomatoes and Worcestershire sauce. Spoon over meat.

3. Arrange vegetables over top.

4. Cover and cook on Low 5–6 hours or until meat and vegetables are tender but not overcooked.

Cal: 180
Fat: 4g
Sodium: 360mg
Carbs: 16g
Sugar: 7g
Protein: 20g

Corned Beef and Cabbage

Carrie Darby, Wayland, IA
Leona Yoder, Hartville, OH
Esther Porter, Minneapolis, MN
Betty K. Drescher, Quakertown, PA
Karen Ceneviva, New Haven, CT
Bonita Ensenberger, Albuquerque, NM
Dorothy Lingerfelt, Stonyford, CA

Makes 6 servings

Prep Time: 30 minutes & *Cooking Time: 4–7 hours* & *Ideal slow-cooker size: 5- or 6-qt.*

3–4-lb. corned beef brisket (not in a brine), cut into 6–8 pieces

¾–1¼ cups water

5–6 carrots, cut in 2–3" pieces

3 medium-sized onions, quartered

salt and pepper

half to a whole head of cabbage, cut into wedges

1. Place corned beef in the slow cooker. Add water.

2. Place carrots and onions around the meat if possible, pushing the vegetables in so they're at least partly covered by the water. Sprinkle salt and pepper over all.

3. Cover and cook on Low 4–5 hours, or on High 2½–3 hours.

4. Add cabbage to cooker, pushing down into liquid to moisten. Turn to High and cook an additional 1½–2 hours, or until vegetables and meat are tender but not overcooked.

Variation:

Add 3 medium-sized potatoes, peeled or unpeeled, cut into chunks, to Step 2.

—Sharon Timpe, Jackson, WI

TIP

You can prepare the cabbage separately in a large soup pot. Place wedges in kettle and add 1 cup broth from cooker. Cook 20 to 30 minutes, covered, or until just-tender. Stir into corned beef and vegetables right before serving.

Cal: 500
Fat: 34g
Sodium: 2810mg
Carbs: 11g
Sugar: 7g
Protein: 34g

PORK

Savory Pork Roast

Mary Louise Martin, Boyd, WI

Makes 4–6 servings
Prep Time: 15 minutes 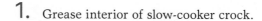 Cooking Time: 3½–4½ hours Ideal slow-cooker size: 6-qt. oval

4-lb. boneless pork butt roast
I tsp. ground ginger
I Tbsp. fresh minced rosemary
½ tsp. mace or nutmeg
I tsp. coarsely ground black pepper
2 tsp. salt
2 cups water

1. Grease interior of slow-cooker crock.

2. Place roast in the slow cooker.

3. In a bowl, mix spices and seasonings together. Sprinkle half on top of roast, pushing down on spices to encourage them to stick.

4. Flip roast and sprinkle with rest of spices, again, pushing down to make them stick.

5. Pour 2 cups water around the edge, being careful not to wash spices off meat.

6. Cover. Cook on Low 3½–4½ hours, or until instant-read meat thermometer registers 140°F when stuck into center of roast.

Calories: 480
Fat: 15g
Sodium: 1100mg
Carbs: .5g
Sugar: 0g
Protein: 81.5g

Cranberry Pork Roast

Chris Peterson, Green Bay, WI
Joyce Kaut, Rochester, NY

Makes 6–8 servings
Prep Time: 5 minutes ⚬ Cooking Time: 6–8 hours ⚬ Ideal slow-cooker size: 5-qt.

3–4-lb. pork roast
salt and pepper to taste
I cup finely chopped cranberries
¼ cup honey
I tsp. grated orange peel
½ tsp. ground nutmeg, *optional*
½ tsp. ground cloves, *optional*

1. Sprinkle roast with salt and pepper. Place in the slow cooker.

2. Combine remaining ingredients in a bowl. Pour over roast.

3. Cover and cook on Low 6–8 hours, or until meat is tender.

Cal: 230
Fat: 3g
Sodium: 85mg
Carbs: 10g
Sugar: 9g
Protein: 39g

Pork and Sweet Potatoes

Vera F. Schmucker, Goshen, IN

Makes 4 servings

Prep Time: 15 minutes ⚬ *Cooking Time: 4–4½ hours* ⚬ *Ideal slow-cooker size: 4-qt.*

4 pork loin chops

salt and pepper to taste

4 sweet potatoes, cut in large chunks

2 onions, cut in quarters

½ cup apple cider

1. Place meat in bottom of slow cooker. Salt and pepper to taste.

2. Arrange sweet potatoes and onions over the pork.

3. Pour apple cider over all.

4. Cook on High 30 minutes and then on Low 3½–4 hours, or until meat and vegetables are tender but not dry.

Cal: 220
Fat: 2g
Sodium: 280mg
Carbs: 31g
Sugar: 8g
Protein: 20g

Pork Chops and Apple Slices

Dorothy VanDeest, Memphis, TN
Dale Peterson, Rapid City, SD

Makes 4 servings
Prep Time: 15 minutes ⚜ *Cooking Time: 6–8 hours* ⚜ *Ideal slow-cooker size: 3- to 4-qt.*

4 pork loin chops, about 1" thick, well trimmed

2 medium-sized apples, peeled, cored, and sliced

1 tsp. coconut oil

¼ tsp. nutmeg, *optional*

salt and pepper to taste

1. Heat a nonstick skillet until hot. Add chops and brown quickly. Turn and brown on the other side.

2. While chops are browning, place half the sliced apples in the slow cooker. Top with 2 chops. Repeat the layers.

3. Dot with coconut oil and sprinkle with nutmeg. Sprinkle generously with salt and pepper.

4. Cover and cook on Low 6–8 hours, or until meat is tender but not dry.

Variation:

Chop one small onion fine. Sprinkle half the onion pieces over the first layer of chops, and the rest of it over the second layer of chops.

—Kate Johnson, Rolfe, IA

Cal: 290
Fat: 8g
Sodium: 115mg
Carbs: 16g
Sugar: 11g
Protein: 38g

Raspberry Balsamic Pork Chops

Hope Comerford, Clinton Township, MI

Makes 4–6 servings
Prep Time: 5 minutes ♣ Cooking Time: 7–8 hours ♣ Ideal slow-cooker size: 3-qt.

4–5 lbs. thick-cut pork chops
¼ cup raspberry balsamic vinegar
2 Tbsp. olive oil
½ tsp. kosher salt
½ tsp. garlic powder
¼ tsp. basil
¼ cup water

1. Place pork chops in the slow cooker.

2. In a small bowl, mix together the remaining ingredients. Pour over the pork chops.

3. Cover and cook on Low for 7–8 hours.

Calories: 475
Fat: 16g
Sodium: 360mg
Carbs: 0g
Sugar: 0g
Protein: 76.5g

Salsa Verde Pork

Hope Comerford, Clinton Township, MI

Makes 6 servings
Prep Time: 20 minutes ⚬ Cooking Time: 6–6½ hours ⚬ Ideal slow-cooker size: 4-qt.

1½-lb. boneless pork loin

1 large sweet onion, halved and sliced

2 large tomatoes, chopped

1 16-oz. jar gluten-free salsa verde
(green salsa)

½ cup dry white wine

4 cloves garlic, minced

1 tsp. cumin

½ tsp. chili powder

1. Place the pork loin in the crock and add the rest of the ingredients on top.

2. Cover and cook on Low for 6–6½ hours.

3. Break apart the pork with 2 forks and mix with contents of crock.

Serving suggestion:

Serve over cooked brown rice or quinoa.

Calories: 230
Fat: 5.5g
Sodium: 525mg
Carbs: 13g
Sugar: 7g
Protein: 27.45g

Carnitas

Hope Comerford, Clinton Township, MI

Makes 12 servings
Prep Time: 10 minutes ☙ Cooking Time: 10–12 hours ☙ Ideal slow-cooker size: 4-qt.

2-lb. pork shoulder roast

1½ tsp. kosher salt

½ tsp. pepper

2 tsp. cumin

5 cloves garlic, minced

1 tsp. oregano

3 bay leaves

2 cups gluten-free, low-sodium chicken stock

2 Tbsp. lime juice

1 tsp. lime zest

1. Place pork shoulder roast in crock.

2. Mix together the salt, pepper, cumin, garlic, and oregano. Rub it onto the pork roast.

3. Place the bay leaves around the pork roast, then pour in the chicken stock around the roast, being careful not to wash off the spices.

4. Cover and cook on Low for 10–12 hours.

5. Remove the roast with a slotted spoon, as well as the bay leaves. Shred the pork between 2 forks, then replace the shredded pork in the crock and stir.

6. Add the lime juice and lime zest to the crock and stir.

7. Serve on warmed white corn tortillas.

Calories: 220
Fat: 8g
Sodium: 390mg
Carbs: 14.5g
Sugar: 1g
Protein: 22.5g

North Carolina Barbecue

J. B. Miller, Indianapolis, IN

Makes 8–12 servings
Prep Time: 15 minutes ☙ *Cooking Time: 5–8 hours* ☙ *Ideal slow-cooker size: 4- to 5-qt.*

3–4-lb. pork loin, roast or shoulder

1 cup apple cider vinegar

¼ cup plus 1 Tbsp. prepared mustard

¼ cup plus 1 Tbsp. gluten-free Worcestershire sauce

2 tsp. red pepper flakes

1. Trim fat from pork. Place in the slow cooker.

2. In a bowl, mix remaining ingredients together. Spoon over meat.

3. Cover and cook on High 5 hours, or Low 8 hours, or until meat is tender but not dry.

4. Slice, or break meat apart, and serve drizzled with the cooking juices. If you use the meat for sandwiches, you'll have enough for 8–12 sandwiches.

Cal: 150
Fat: 4.5g
Sodium: 220mg
Carbs: 3g
Sugar: 1g
Protein: 24g

Italian Country-Style Pork Ribs

Kay Kassinger, Port Angeles, WA

Makes 8–10 servings
Prep Time: 20 minutes   ♣   Cooking Time: 7–8 hours   ♣   Ideal slow-cooker size: 5-qt.

3–3½ lbs. country-style pork ribs, cut into serving-size pieces

2 14½-oz. cans Italian-seasoned diced tomatoes

1 cup frozen pearl onions

1½ tsp. Italian seasoning

1 tsp. salt

water as needed

1. Brown ribs on top and bottom in nonstick skillet. Do in batches to assure that each piece browns well.

2. Spray cooker with nonstick cooking spray. Transfer browned meat to the slow cooker.

3. Drain tomatoes into hot skillet. Deglaze skillet with tomato juice by stirring up the drippings with a wooden spoon.

4. Layer tomatoes, onions, and seasonings over the ribs. Pour deglazed pan drippings into the slow cooker. Add about 2" of water.

5. Cover and cook on Low 7–8 hours, or until meat is tender but not overcooked.

Cal: 240
Fat: 9g
Sodium: 220mg
Carbs: 4g
Sugar: 2g
Protein: 34g

Ham and Cabbage

Tim Smith, Rutledge, PA

Makes 4 servings
Prep Time: 30 minutes ❧ Cooking Time: 6–7 hours ❧ Ideal slow-cooker size: 6- to 7-qt.

2 lbs. ham, uncooked
12 whole cloves
8 medium-sized red potatoes
1 medium-sized head green cabbage
water

1. Rinse ham, then stick cloves evenly into ham. Place in center of slow cooker.

2. Cut potatoes in half. Add to the slow cooker around the ham.

3. Quarter cabbage and remove center stem. Add to cooker, again surrounding the ham.

4. Fill with water to cover.

5. Cover and cook on High for 6–7 hours, or until vegetables and meat are tender, but not dry or mushy.

Serving Suggestion:

Serve with mustard for the ham and butter for the potatoes.

Cal: 580
Fat: 19g
Sodium: 6170mg
Carbs: 32g
Sugar: 9g
Protein: 68g

Sausage and Green Beans

Joy Yoder, Harrisonburg, VA

Makes 6 servings
Prep Time: 15 minutes   Cooking Time: 2–5 hours   Ideal slow-cooker size: 3- to 4-qt.

1½ lbs. link sausage, cut into 2" pieces
1 qt. green beans, frozen
1 apple, diced or sliced with peel
1 cup water

1. Place sausage in the slow cooker.

2. Add beans, apple, and water. Mix together well.

3. Cover and cook on High 2 hours, or on Low 4–5 hours, or until sausage and beans are both tender.

Cal: 470
Fat: 42g
Sodium: 920mg
Carbs: 6g
Sugar: 3g
Protein: 17g

CHICKEN/TURKEY

Chicken Pot Roast

Carol Eberly, Harrisonburg, VA
Sarah Miller, Harrisonburg, VA

Makes 4 servings
Prep Time: 10–15 minutes ⚜ Cooking Time: 3–4 hours ⚜ Ideal slow-cooker size: 4- to 5-qt.

4 boneless, skinless chicken breast halves

salt and pepper to taste

4–6 medium-sized carrots, peeled and sliced

2 cups lima beans, fresh or frozen

1 cup water

1. Salt and pepper chicken breasts. Place chicken in the slow cooker and start cooking on High.

2. Prepare carrots and place on top of chicken. Add limas on top. Pour water over all.

3. Cover and cook on Low 3–4 hours, or until chicken and vegetables are tender but not dry or mushy.

Serving Suggestion:

Serve over rice.

Cal: 420
Fat: 7g
Sodium: 200mg
Carbs: 26g
Sugar: 6g
Protein: 60g

Roast Chicken

Betty Drescher, Quakertown, PA

Makes 6 servings

Prep Time: 30 minutes ⚜ *Cooking Time: 9–11 hours* ⚜ *Ideal slow-cooker size: 4- to 5-qt.*

3–4-lb. roasting chicken or hen
1 ½ tsp. salt
¼ tsp. pepper
1 tsp. parsley flakes, *divided*
1 Tbsp. olive oil
½–1 cup water

1. Thoroughly wash chicken and pat dry.

2. Sprinkle cavity with salt, pepper, and ½ tsp. parsley flakes. Place in the slow cooker, breast side up.

3. Rub or brush chicken with olive oil.

4. Sprinkle with remaining parsley flakes. Add water around the chicken.

5. Cover and cook on High 1 hour. Turn to Low and cook 8–10 hours.

TIPS

1. Sprinkle with basil or tarragon in Step 4, if you wish.

2. To make it a more complete meal, put carrots, onions, and celery in the bottom of the slow cooker.

Cal: 270
Fat: 8g
Sodium: 400mg
Carbs: 0g
Sugar: 0g
Protein: 45g

Herby Chicken

Joyce Bowman, Lady Lake, FL

Makes 4–6 servings
Prep Time: 10 minutes ⚘ *Cooking Time: 5–7 hours* ⚘ *Ideal slow-cooker size: 5-qt.*

2½–3½-lb. whole roaster chicken

I lemon, cut into wedges

I bay leaf

2–4 sprigs fresh thyme,
or ¾ tsp. dried thyme

salt and pepper to taste

1. Remove giblets from chicken.

2. Put lemon wedges and bay leaf in cavity.

3. Place whole chicken in the slow cooker.

4. Scatter sprigs of thyme over the chicken. Sprinkle with salt and pepper.

5. Cover and cook on Low 5–7 hours, or until chicken is tender.

Serving Suggestion:

Serve hot with pasta or rice, or debone and freeze for your favorite casseroles or salads.

Cal: 210
Fat: 5g
Sodium: 140mg
Carbs: 2g
Sugar: 0g
Protein: 39g

Poached Chicken

Mary E. Wheatley, Mashpee, MA

Makes 6 servings
Prep Time: 15 minutes ⚶ Cooking Time: 7–8 hours ⚶ Ideal slow-cooker size: 4½-qt.

1 whole broiler-fryer chicken, about 3 lbs.

1 celery rib, cut into chunks

1 carrot, sliced

1 medium-sized onion, sliced

1 cup low-sodium, gluten-free chicken broth, seasoned, or water

1. Wash chicken. Pat dry with paper towels and place in the slow cooker.

2. Place celery, carrot, and onion around chicken. Pour broth over all.

3. Cover and cook on Low 7–8 hours, or until chicken is tender.

4. Remove chicken from pot and place on platter. When cool enough to handle, debone.

5. Strain broth into a container and chill.

6. Place chunks of meat in fridge or freezer until ready to use in salads or main dishes.

Cal: 120
Fat: 3.5g
Sodium: 150mg
Carbs: 4g
Sugar: 2g
Protein: 17g

Chicken with Vegetables

Janie Steele, Moore, OK

Makes 4 servings
Prep Time: 10–15 minutes   ♣   *Cooking Time: 6–8 hours*   ♣   *Ideal slow-cooker size: 6-qt.*

4 bone-in chicken breast halves

1 small head of cabbage, quartered

1-lb. pkg. baby carrots

2 14½-oz. cans Mexican-flavored stewed tomatoes with juice

1. Place all ingredients in the slow cooker in order listed.

2. Cover and cook on Low 6–8 hours, or until chicken and vegetables are tender.

Cal: 440
Fat: 7g
Sodium: 680mg
Carbs: 37g
Sugar: 20g
Protein: 59g

Honey Baked Chicken

Mary Kennell, Roanoke, IL

Makes 4 servings
Prep Time: 15 minutes & Cooking Time: 3–6 hours & Ideal slow-cooker size: 5-qt.

4 skinless, bone-in chicken breast halves

2 Tbsp. coconut oil, melted

2 Tbsp. honey

2 tsp. prepared mustard

2 tsp. curry powder

salt and pepper, *optional*

1. Spray slow cooker with nonstick cooking spray and add chicken.

2. Mix coconut oil, honey, mustard, and curry powder together in a small bowl. Pour sauce over chicken.

3. Cover and cook on High 3 hours, or on Low 5–6 hours.

Variations:

1. Use chicken thighs instead of breasts. Drop the curry powder if you wish.

   —Cathy Boshart, Lebanon, PA

2. Use a small fryer chicken, quartered, instead of breasts or thighs.

   —Frances Kruba, Dundalk, MD

3. Instead of curry powder, use ½ tsp. paprika.

   —Jena Hammond, Traverse City, MI

Cal: 380
Fat: 7g
Sodium: 135mg
Carbs: 9g
Sugar: 9g
Protein: 53g

Lemon Pepper Chicken with Veggies

Nadine Martinitz, Salina KS

Makes 4 servings

Prep Time: 20 minutes ♣ Cooking Time: 4–10 hours ♣ Ideal slow-cooker size: 4-qt.

4 carrots, sliced ½" thick

4 potatoes, cut in 1" chunks

2 cloves garlic, peeled and minced, *optional*

4 whole chicken legs and thighs, skin removed

2 tsp. lemon pepper seasoning

1¾ cup low-sodium, gluten-free chicken broth

1. Layer vegetables and chicken in the slow cooker.

2. Sprinkle with lemon pepper seasoning. Pour broth over all.

3. Cover and cook on Low 8–10 hours or on High 4–5 hours.

Variation:

Add 2 cups frozen green beans to the bottom layer (Step 1) in the cooker.

—Earnest Zimmerman, Mechanicsburg, PA

Cal: 240
Fat: 8g
Sodium: 290mg
Carbs: 19g
Sugar: 5g
Protein: 21g

Juicy Orange Chicken

Andrea Maher, Dunedin, FL

Makes 6 servings
Prep Time: 10 minutes & Cooking Time: 6–8 hours & Ideal slow-cooker size: 5- or 6-qt.

18–24 oz. boneless, skinless chicken breast, cut into small pieces

1 cup orange juice, no additives

¼ cup honey

6 small oranges, peeled and sliced

¼ cup Bragg's liquid aminos

1. Add all the ingredients to the slow cooker.

2. Cover and cook on High 3–4 hours or Low 6–8 hours.

Serving suggestion:

Serve over Broccoli Slaw.

Calories: 240
Fat: 2g
Sodium: 730mg
Carbs: 33g
Sugar: 25g
Protein: 26g

Garlic and Lemon Chicken

Hope Comerford, Clinton Township, MI

Makes 5 servings
Prep Time: 5 minutes ❧ *Cooking Time: 5–6 hours* ❧ *Ideal slow-cooker size: 3- or 5-qt.*

4–5 lbs. boneless, skinless chicken breasts or thighs

½ cup minced shallots

½ cup olive oil

¼ cup lemon juice

1 Tbsp. garlic paste (or use 1 medium clove garlic, minced)

1 Tbsp. no-salt seasoning

⅛ tsp. pepper

1. Place chicken in the slow cooker.

2. In a small bowl, mix the remaining ingredients. Pour this mixture over the chicken in the crock.

3. Cover and cook on Low for 5–6 hours.

Calories: 450
Fat: 9g
Sodium: 260mg
Carbs: 3g
Sugar: 0g
Protein: 87g

That's Amore Chicken Cacciatore

Carol Sherwood, Batavia, NY

Makes 6 servings
Prep Time: 20 minutes ☙ Cooking Time: 7–9 hours ☙ Ideal slow-cooker size: 6-qt.

6 boneless, skinless chicken breast halves, *divided*

28-oz. jar low-sugar, low-sodium spaghetti sauce

2 green peppers, chopped

1 onion, minced

2 Tbsp. minced garlic

1. Place a layer of chicken in your slow cooker.

2. Mix remaining ingredients together in a bowl. Spoon half of the sauce over the first layer of chicken.

3. Add remaining breast halves. Top with remaining sauce.

4. Cover and cook on Low 7–9 hours, or until chicken is tender but not dry.

Serving Suggestion:

Serve with cooked spaghetti or linguine.

Cal: 340
Fat: 7g
Sodium: 125mg
Carbs: 13g
Sugar: 7g
Protein: 56g

Spanish Chicken

Natalia Showalter, Mt. Solon, VA

Makes 4–6 servings
Prep Time: 15–20 minutes ⚜ Cooking Time: 5–6 hours ⚜ Ideal slow-cooker size: 3- to 6-qt.

8 chicken thighs, skinned

½–1 cup red wine vinegar, according to your taste preference

⅔ cups tamari, or low-sodium soy sauce

1 tsp. garlic powder

4 6" cinnamon sticks

1. Brown chicken slightly in nonstick skillet, if you wish, and then transfer to greased slow cooker.

2. Mix wine vinegar, tamari sauce, and garlic powder together in a bowl. Pour over chicken.

3. Break cinnamon sticks into several pieces and distribute among chicken thighs.

4. Cover and cook on Low 5–6 hours, or until chicken is tender but not dry.

TIP
You can skip browning the chicken if you're in a hurry, but browning it gives the finished dish a better flavor.

Cal: 360
Fat: 34g
Sodium: 1180mg
Carbs: 2g
Sugar: 0g
Protein: 10g

Italian Crockpot Chicken

Andrea Maher, Dunedin, FL

Makes 6 servings

Prep Time: 5 minutes ❧ *Cooking Time: 6–8 hours* ❧ *Ideal slow-cooker size: 6-qt.*

24 oz. boneless skinless chicken breast, cut into small pieces

3 cups garbanzo beans

16-oz. bag frozen spinach

2 cups mushrooms

2 Tbsp. Mrs. Dash Italian seasoning

1 cup low-sodium, gluten-free chicken broth

1. Add all ingredients to the slow cooker.

2. Cover and cook on Low for 6–8 hours or High for 3–4 hours.

Calories: 280
Fat: 4g
Sodium: 270mg
Carbs: 25g
Sugar: 4g
Protein: 34g

Curried Chicken Dinner

Janessa Hochstedler, East Earl, PA

Makes 6 servings
Prep Time: 20 minutes ⚹ Cooking Time: 5–10 hours ⚹ Ideal slow-cooker size: 3-qt.

1½ lbs. boneless, skinless chicken thighs, quartered

3 potatoes, peeled and cut into chunks, about 2 cups

1 apple, chopped

2 Tbsp. curry powder

1¾ cup low-sodium, gluten-free chicken broth

1 medium-sized onion, chopped, *optional*

1. Place all ingredients in the slow cooker. Mix together gently.

2. Cover and cook on Low 8–10 hours or on High 5 hours, or until chicken is tender, but not dry.

3. Serve over cooked rice.

Cal: 560
Fat: 51g
Sodium: 135mg
Carbs: 13g
Sugar: 5g
Protein: 13g

Stewed Oriental Chicken

Stanley Kropf, Elkhart, IN

Makes 4–6 servings
Prep Time: 15–20 minutes ♣ Cooking Time: 4 hours ♣ Ideal slow-cooker size: 4- to 5-qt.

1 whole chicken, cut up

3 Tbsp. hot sweet mustard, or 2 Tbsp. hot mustard and 1 Tbsp. honey

2 Tbsp. low-sodium, gluten-free soy sauce or liquid aminos

1 tsp. ground ginger

1 tsp. cumin

1. Wash chicken and place in the slow cooker. Pat dry.

2. Mix the remaining ingredients in a bowl. Taste and adjust seasonings if you want. Pour over chicken.

3. Cover and cook on High for at least 4 hours, or until tender. If it's more convenient, you can cook the meat an hour or so longer with no negative effect.

TIPS

1. This is a folk recipe, so the cook should experiment to taste. I often use a variety of optional ingredients, depending on how I'm feeling. These include teriyaki sauce, oyster sauce, cardamom, sesame and olive oil, dry vermouth, and garlic, in whatever amount and combination seems right.

2. If you cook the dish longer than 4 hours, the chicken tends to fall apart. In any event, serve it in a bowl large enough to hold the chiken and broth.

3. I like to serve this with cooked plain or saffron rice.

Cal: 110
Fat: 3.5g
Sodium: 100mg
Carbs: 1g
Sugar: 1g
Protein: 16g

Thai Chicken

Joanne Good, Wheaton, IL

Makes 6 servings

Prep Time: 5 minutes   Cooking Time: 8–9 hours   Ideal slow-cooker size: 4-qt.

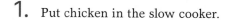

6 skinless chicken thighs

¾ cup gluten-free salsa,
your choice of mild, medium, or hot

¼ cup chunky all-natural peanut butter

1 Tbsp. low-sodium, gluten-free
soy sauce or liquid aminos

2 Tbsp. lime juice

1 tsp. gingerroot, grated, *optional*

2 Tbsp. cilantro, chopped, *optional*

1 Tbsp. dry-roasted peanuts,
chopped, *optional*

1. Put chicken in the slow cooker.

2. In a bowl, mix remaining ingredients together, except cilantro and chopped peanuts.

3. Cover and cook on Low 8–9 hours, or until chicken is cooked through but not dry.

4. Skim off any fat. Remove chicken to a platter and serve topped with sauce. Sprinkle with peanuts and cilantro, if you wish.

5. Serve over cooked rice.

Variation:

Vegetarians can substitute 2 15-oz. cans of white beans, and perhaps some tempeh, for the chicken.

Cal: 260
Fat: 26g
Sodium: 115mg
Carbs: 2g
Sugar: 0g
Protein: 6g

Simple Savory Chicken

Hope Comerford, Clinton Township, MI

Makes 4–6 servings
Prep Time: 5–8 minutes ♣ Cooking Time: 7–8 hours ♣ Ideal slow-cooker size: 3-qt.

2 lbs. skinless chicken leg quarters

¼ cup chopped onion

2 cloves garlic, minced

1 tsp. basil

1 tsp. dill

½ tsp. salt

¼ tsp. black pepper

1 cup water

2 Tbsp. apple cider vinegar

1. Place the chicken in the crock. Sprinkle with the onion and garlic.

2. In a bowl, mix together the basil, dill, salt, and pepper. Sprinkle this evenly over the chicken.

3. Pour in the water and apple cider vinegar around the chicken, being careful not to wash off the spices.

4. Cover and cook on Low for 7–8 hours.

Calories: 225
Fat: 7.5g
Sodium: 410mg
Carbs: 1.5g
Sugar: .5g
Protein: 35g

Greek Chicken Pita Filling

Judi Manos, Wist Islip, NY
Jeanette Oberholtzer, Manheim, PA

Makes 4 servings
Prep Time: 10 minutes   ❧   Cooking Time: 6–8 hours   ❧   Ideal slow-cooker size: 2- to 3-qt.

1 onion, chopped
1 lb. boneless, skinless chicken thighs
1 tsp. lemon pepper
½ tsp. dried oregano
½ cup plain yogurt

1. Combine first 3 ingredients in the slow cooker. Cover and cook on Low 6–8 hours, or until chicken is tender.

2. Just before serving, remove chicken and shred with two forks.

3. Add shredded chicken back into the slow cooker and stir in oregano and yogurt.

4. Serve as a filling for pita bread.

Cal: 470
Fat: 44g
Sodium: 170mg
Carbs: 4g
Sugar: 3g
Protein: 14g

Easy Enchilada Shredded Chicken

Hope Comerford, Clinton Township, MI

Makes 10–14 servings
Prep Time: 5 minutes ⚭ Cooking Time: 5–6 hours ⚭ Ideal slow-cooker size: 3- or 5-qt.

5–6 lbs. boneless, skinless chicken breast

14.5-oz. can low-sodium petite diced tomatoes

1 medium onion, chopped

8 oz. gluten-free red enchilada sauce

½ tsp. salt

½ tsp. chili powder

½ tsp. basil

½ tsp. garlic powder

¼ tsp. pepper

1. Place chicken in the crock.

2. Add in the remaining ingredients.

3. Cover and cook on Low for 5–6 hours.

4. Remove chicken and shred it between two forks. Place the shredded chicken back in the crock and stir to mix in the juices.

Serving suggestion:

Serve over salad, brown rice, quinoa, sweet potatoes, nachos, or soft corn tortillas. Add a dollop of yogurt and a sprinkle of fresh cilantro.

Calories: 240
Fat: 5g
Sodium: 340mg
Carbs: 4g
Sugar: 2g
Protein: 44g

Chicken Curry with Rice

Jennifer Yoder Sommers, Harrisonburg, VA

Makes 6 servings
Prep Time: 10 minutes ❧ Cooking Time: 5–10 hours ❧ Ideal slow-cooker size: 3- to 4-qt.

1½ lbs. boneless, skinless chicken thighs, quartered

1 onion, chopped

2 cups uncooked long-grain rice

2 Tbsp. curry powder

1¾ cups gluten-free, low-sodium chicken broth

1. Combine all ingredients in your slow cooker.

2. Cover and cook on Low 8–10 hours, or on High 5 hours, or until chicken is tender but not dry.

Variation:

Add 1 chopped apple to Step 1. Thirty minutes before the end of the cooking time, stir in 2 cups frozen peas.

Cal: 760
Fat: 52g
Sodium: 160mg
Carbs: 55g
Sugar: 2g
Protein: 18g

Spicy Chicken

Joan Miller, Wayland, IA

Makes 10 servings
Prep Time: 15–20 minutes ❧ *Cooking Time: 3–4½ hours* ❧ *Ideal slow-cooker size: 4- to 5-qt.*

10 skinless, bone-in chicken breast halves, *divided*

16-oz. jar gluten-free salsa, mild, medium, or hot

1 medium-sized onion, chopped

2 Tbsp. curry powder

1 cup nonfat plain Greek yogurt

1. Place half the chicken in the slow cooker.

2. Combine salsa, onion, and curry powder in a medium-sized bowl. Pour half the sauce over the meat in the cooker.

3. Repeat Steps 1 and 2.

4. Cover and cook on High for 3 hours. Or cook on High for 1½ hours, and then turn cooker to Low and cook 3 more hours.

5. Remove chicken to serving platter and cover to keep warm.

6. Add nonfat plain Greek yogurt to the slow cooker and stir into salsa until well blended. Serve over the chicken.

Serving Suggestion:

Great served over rice.

Cal: 320
Fat: 6g
Sodium: 340mg
Carbs: 5g
Sugar: 3g
Protein: 56g

Slow-cooker Turkey Breast

Liz Ann Yoder, Hartville, OH

Makes 8–10 servings

Prep Time: 10 minutes ⚜ *Cooking Time: 9–10 hours* ⚜ *Ideal slow-cooker size: 6- to 7-qt.*

6-lb. turkey breast
2 tsp. olive oil
salt to taste
pepper to taste
1 medium onion, quartered
4 garlic cloves, peeled
½ cup water

1. Rinse turkey and pat dry with paper towels.

2. Rub oil over turkey. Sprinkle with salt and pepper. Place, meaty side up, in large slow cooker.

3. Place onion and garlic around sides of cooker. Add water.

4. Cover. Cook on Low 9–10 hours, or until meat thermometer stuck in meaty part of breast registers 180°.

5. Remove from the slow cooker and let stand 10 minutes before slicing.

6. Serve with mashed potatoes, cranberry salad, and corn or green beans.

Cal: 440
Fat: 21g
Sodium: 200mg
Carbs: 1g
Sugar: 0g
Protein: 60g

Thyme and Garlic Turkey Breast

Hope Comerford, Clinton Township, MI

Makes 6–8 servings
Prep Time: 10 minutes ♣ Cooking Time: 7–8 hours ♣ Ideal slow-cooker size: 6- or 7-qt.

4 lb. bone-in turkey breast, giblets removed if there are any, skin removed, washed, and patted dry

¼ cup olive oil

1 Tbsp. balsamic vinegar

1 Tbsp. water

1 orange, juiced

6 cloves garlic, minced

1½ tsp. dried thyme

1 tsp. onion powder

1 tsp. kosher salt

1. Place turkey breast in crock.

2. Mix together the remaining ingredients and pour over the turkey breast. Rub it in on all sides with clean hands.

3. Cover and cook on Low for 7–8 hours.

Calories: 360
Fat: 11.5g
Sodium: 610mg
Carbs: 3.5g
Sugar: 1.5g
Protein: 58g

Moist and Tender Turkey Breast

Marlene Weaver, Lititz, PA

Makes 12 servings
Prep Time: 10 minutes ⚶ *Cooking Time: 4–6 hours* ⚶ *Ideal slow-cooker size: 6- or 7-qt.*

I bone-in turkey breast (6–7 lbs.)
4 fresh rosemary sprigs
4 garlic cloves, peeled
I Tbsp. brown sugar
½ tsp. coarsely ground pepper
¼ tsp. salt

1. Place turkey in a crock and place rosemary and garlic around it.

2. Combine the brown sugar, pepper, and salt; sprinkle over turkey.

3. Cover and cook on Low for 4–6 hours or until turkey is tender.

Sage Turkey Thighs

Carolyn Baer, Conrath, WI

Makes 4 servings
Prep Time: 15 minutes ⚘ *Cooking Time: 6–8 hours* ⚘ *Ideal slow-cooker size: 3-qt.*

4 medium-sized carrots, halved

1 medium-sized onion, chopped

½ cup water

1½ tsp. dried sage, *divided*

2 skinless turkey thighs or drumsticks, about 2 lbs.

1 tsp. browning sauce, *optional*

¼ tsp. salt, *optional*

⅓ tsp. pepper, *optional*

1 Tbsp. cornstarch, *optional*

¼ cup water, *optional*

1. In a slow cooker, combine the carrots, onion, water, and 1 tsp. sage. Top with the turkey. Sprinkle with the remaining sage.

2. Cover and cook on Low 6–8 hours, or until a meat thermometer reads 180°.

3. Remove turkey and keep warm. Remove vegetables from the cooker with a slotted spoon, reserving cooking juices.

4. Keep vegetables warm until ready to serve. Pour cooking juices into a saucepan.

5. Or, place vegetables in a food processor. Cover and process until smooth. Place in a saucepan. Add cooking juices.

6. Bring mixture in saucepan to a boil. Add browning sauce, salt, and pepper, if you wish.

7. In a small bowl, combine cornstarch and water until smooth. Stir into boiling juices. Cook and stir for 2 minutes, or until thickened. Serve over turkey.

8. If you've kept the vegetables warm, add to the serving platter with the turkey.

TIP
Add a little minced garlic to Step 1 if you wish.

Cal: 230
Fat: 5g
Sodium: 270mg
Carbs: 8g
Sugar: 4g
Protein: 40g

Indonesian Turkey

Elaine Sue Good, Tiskilwa, IL

Makes 4 servings
Prep Time: 10 minutes ❧ *Cooking Time: 6–8 hours* ❧ *Ideal slow-cooker size: 2- to 3½-qt.*

3 turkey breast tenderloins (about 1½–2 lbs.)

6 cloves garlic, pressed and chopped

1½ Tbsp. grated fresh ginger

1 Tbsp. sesame oil

3 Tbsp. low-sodium, gluten-free soy sauce or liquid aminos, *optional*

½ tsp. cayenne pepper, *optional*

⅓ cup all-natural peanut butter, your choice of chunky or smooth

1. Place the turkey on the bottom of your slow cooker.

2. Sprinkle with garlic, ginger, and sesame oil.

3. Cover and cook on Low 8 hours or until meat thermometer registers 180°.

4. With a slotted spoon, remove turkey pieces from the slow cooker. Stir peanut butter into remaining juices. If the sauce is thicker than you like, stir in ¼–⅓ cup water.

5. Spoon peanut butter sauce over turkey to serve.

TIPS

1. If you like spicier foods, be sure to include the cayenne pepper and add it as part of Step 2. And, if your diet allows, add the soy sauce during Step 2 also.

2. You may substitute 4 whole boneless, skinless chicken breasts or 12 boneless, skinless chicken thighs for the 3 turkey breast tenderloins. I have used both and was pleased with the results.

3. The more meat you have the more evenly it will cook, especially if your slow cooker cooks hot.

Cal: 330
Fat: 17g
Sodium: 450mg
Carbs: 7g
Sugar: 2g
Protein: 42g

Turkey with Mushroom Sauce

Judi Manos, West Islip, NY

Makes 12 servings
Prep Time: 25 minutes   ⚘   Cooking Time: 7–8 hours   ⚘   Ideal slow-cooker size: 6-qt.

1 large boneless, skinless turkey breast, halved

2 Tbsp. melted coconut oil

2 Tbsp. dried parsley

½ tsp. dried oregano

½ tsp. kosher salt

¼ tsp. black pepper

½ cup white wine

1 cup fresh mushrooms, sliced

2 Tbsp. cornstarch

¼ cup cold water

1. Place turkey in the slow cooker. Brush with coconut oil.

2. Mix together parsley, oregano, salt, pepper, and wine. Pour over turkey.

3. Top with mushrooms.

4. Cover and cook on Low for 7–8 hours or just until turkey is tender.

5. Remove turkey and keep warm.

6. Skim any fat from cooking juices.

7. In a saucepan over low heat combine cornstarch and water and mix until smooth. Gradually add cooking juices from the crock. Bring to a boil. Cook and stir 2 minutes until thickened.

8. Slice turkey and serve with sauce.

Calories: 200
Fat: 4.5g
Sodium: 265mg
Carbs: 2g
Sugar: .5g
Protein: 35g

MEATLESS AND SEAFOOD

Faked You Out Alfredo

Sue Hamilton, Benson, AZ

Makes 4 servings
Prep Time: 5 minutes 🔹 Cooking Time: 6 hours 🔹 Ideal slow-cooker size: 3-qt.

1 lb. bag of frozen cauliflower

1 13½-oz. can light coconut milk

½ cup diced onion

2 cloves garlic, minced

1 Tbsp. vegetable stock concentrate

Salt and pepper to taste

1. Place the frozen cauliflower, coconut milk, onion, garlic, and the vegetable stock concentrate in your crock. Stir mixture to blend in the stock concentrate.

2. Cover and cook on Low for 6 hours.

3. Place cooked mixture in blender and process until smooth.

4. Add salt and pepper to taste.

Variation:

Add cooked peas to sauce after pureeing other ingredients.

Serving suggestion:

Serve over cooked pasta, cooked sliced potatoes, or any other vegetable.

TIP
My husband loves this on pasta with cooked mushrooms mixed in. This sauce can be made ahead of time and refrigerated.

Calories: 205
Fat: 5g
Sodium: 300mg
Carbs: 36g
Sugar: 7g
Protein: 7g

Spiced Cod

Hope Comerford, Clinton Township, MI

Makes 4–6 servings
Prep Time: 8 minutes ⚜ *Cooking Time: 2 hours* ⚜ *Ideal slow-cooker size: 4- or 5-qt.*

4–6 cod fillets
½ cup thinly sliced red onion
1½ tsp. garlic powder
1½ tsp. onion powder
½ tsp. cumin
¼ tsp. Ancho chile
1 lime, juiced
⅓ cup vegetable broth

1. Place fish in the crock. Place the onion on top.

2. Mix together the remaining ingredients and pour over the fish.

3. Cover and cook on Low for 2 hours, or until fish flakes easily with a fork.

Serving suggestion:

Serve on a bed of quinoa or brown rice.

Calories: 200
Fat: 1.5g
Sodium: 190mg
Carbs: 3.5g
Sugar: 1g
Protein: 41.5g

Lemon Dijon Fish

June S. Groff, Denver, PA

Makes 4 servings
Prep Time: 10 minutes ❧ *Cooking Time: 3 hours* ❧ *Ideal slow-cooker size: 2-qt.*

1½ lbs. orange roughy fillets
2 Tbsp. gluten-free Dijon mustard
3 Tbsp. coconut oil, melted
1 tsp. gluten-free Worcestershire sauce
1 Tbsp. lemon juice

1. Cut fillets to fit in the slow cooker.

2. In a bowl, mix remaining ingredients together. Pour sauce over fish. (If you have to stack the fish, spoon a portion of the sauce over the first layer of fish before adding the second layer.)

3. Cover and cook on Low 3 hours, or until fish flakes easily but is not dry or overcooked.

Cal: 220
Fat: 11g
Sodium: 230mg
Carbs: 1g
Sugar: 0g
Protein: 26g

Side Dishes and Vegetables

Orange-Glazed Carrots

Cyndie Marrara, Port Matilda, PA

Makes 6 servings

Prep Time: 5–10 minutes ❧ Cooking Time: 3–4 hours ❧ Ideal slow-cooker size: 3½-qt.

32-oz. (2 lbs.) pkg. baby carrots

⅓ cup turbinado sugar

2–3 oranges, squeezed for juice to make approx. ½ cup juice

3 Tbsp. coconut oil, melted

¾ tsp. cinnamon

¼ tsp. nutmeg

2 Tbsp. cornstarch

¼ cup water

1. Combine all ingredients except cornstarch and water in the slow cooker.

2. Cover. Cook on Low 3–4 hours, until carrots are tender crisp.

3. Put carrots in serving dish and keep warm, reserving cooking juices. Put reserved juices in small saucepan. Bring to boil.

4. Mix cornstarch and water in small bowl until blended. Add to juices. Boil one minute or until thickened, stirring constantly.

5. Pour over carrots and serve.

Serving suggestion:

Sprinkle with orange zest before serving.

Calories: 170
Fat: 7g
Sodium: 120mg
Carbs: 27.5g
Sugar: 19g
Protein: 1g

Slow-cooked Glazed Carrots

Michele Ruvola, Selden, NY

Makes 6–7 servings
Prep Time: 5 minutes ⚘ Cooking Time: 6½–8½ hours ⚘ Ideal slow-cooker size: 3- to 4-qt.

2-lb. bag baby carrots
1½ cups water
¼ cup honey
2 Tbsp. coconut oil
¼ tsp. salt
⅛ tsp. pepper

1. Combine carrots and water in the slow cooker.

2. Cover and cook on Low 6–8 hours, or until carrots are tender.

3. Drain carrots and return to the slow cooker.

4. Stir in honey, coconut oil, salt, and pepper. Mix well.

5. Cover and cook on Low 30 minutes, or until glazed.

Cal: 140
Fat: 5g
Sodium: 150mg
Carbs: 26g
Sugar: 19g
Protein: 1g

Steamed Carrots

Dede Peterson, Rapid City, SD

Makes 4 servings

Prep Time: 15–20 minutes ⚜ *Cooking Time: 4–6 hours* ⚜ *Ideal slow-cooker size: 4-qt.*

8 large carrots, sliced diagonally

¼ cup water

2 Tbsp. coconut oil

1 tsp. turbinado sugar

¼ tsp. salt

1. Layer carrots in the slow cooker. Add water and coconut oil. Sprinkle with sugar and salt.

2. Cover and cook on Low 4–6 hours.

Cal: 110

Fat: 7g

Sodium: 150mg

Carbs: 13g

Sugar: 7g

Protein: 1g

Fresh Green Beans

Lizzie Ann Yoder, Hartville, OH

Makes 6–8 servings
Prep Time: 20 minutes ⚜ *Cooking Time: 6–24 hours* ⚜ *Ideal slow-cooker size: 4- to 5-qt.*

¼ lb. ham or bacon pieces

2 lbs. fresh green beans, washed and cut into pieces, or Frenched

3–4 cups water

1 scant tsp. salt

1. If using bacon, cut it into squares and brown in nonstick skillet. When crispy, drain and set aside.

2. Place all ingredients in the slow cooker. Mix together well.

3. Cover and cook on High 6-10 hours, or on Low 10-24 hours, or until beans are done to your liking.

Cal: 60
Fat: 1g
Sodium: 250mg
Carbs: 8g
Sugar: 4g
Protein: 5g

Greek-Style Green Beans

Diann J. Dunham, State College, PA

Makes 6 servings
Prep Time: 5 minutes ⚶ Cooking Time: 2–5 hours ⚶ Ideal slow-cooker size: 4-qt.

20 ozs. whole or cut-up frozen beans
(not French cut)

2 cups low-sodium tomato sauce

2 tsp. dried onion flakes, *optional*

pinch of dried marjoram or oregano

pinch of ground nutmeg

pinch of cinnamon

1. Combine all ingredients in the slow cooker, mixing together thoroughly.

2. Cover and cook on Low 2–4 hours if the beans are defrosted, or for 3–5 hours on Low if the beans are frozen, or until the beans are done to your liking.

Cal: 45
Fat: 0g
Sodium: 10mg
Carbs: 9g
Sugar: 5g
Protein: 2g

Lemony Garlic Asparagus

Hope Comerford, Clinton Township, MI

Makes 4 servings
Prep Time: 5 minutes & Cooking Time: 1½–2 hours & Ideal slow-cooker size: 2- or 3-qt.

1 lb. asparagus, bottom inch (tough part) removed

1 Tbsp. olive oil

1 ½ Tbsp. lemon juice

3–4 cloves garlic, peeled and minced

¼ tsp. salt

⅛ tsp. pepper

1. Spray crock with nonstick spray.

2. Lay asparagus at bottom of crock and coat with the olive oil.

3. Pour the lemon juice over the top, then sprinkle with the garlic, salt, and pepper.

4. Cover and cook on Low for 1½–2 hours.

Serving suggestion:

Garnish with diced pimento, garlic, and lemon zest.

Calories: 60
Fat: 3.5g
Sodium: 150mg
Carbs: 5.5g
Sugar: 2.5g
Protein: 2.5g

Broccoli and Bell Peppers

Frieda Weisz, Aberdeen, SD

Makes 8 servings
Prep Time: 20 minutes ⚜ *Cooking Time: 4–5 hours* ⚜ *Ideal slow-cooker size: 3½- or 4-qt.*

2 lbs. fresh broccoli, trimmed and chopped into bite-sized pieces

1 clove garlic, minced

1 green or red bell pepper, cut into thin slices

1 onion, peeled and cut into slices

4 Tbsp. low-sodium gluten-free soy sauce or Bragg's liquid aminos

½ tsp. salt

dash of black pepper

1 Tbsp. sesame seeds, *optional*, as garnish

1. Combine all ingredients except sesame seeds in the slow cooker.

2. Cook on Low for 4–5 hours. Top with sesame seeds.

Serving suggestion:

Serve over cooked brown rice.

Calories: 60
Fat: .5g
Sodium: 690mg
Carbs: 10.5g
Sugar: 3.5g
Protein: 4.5g

Brussels Sprouts with Pimentos

Donna Lantgon, Rapid City, SD

Makes 8 servings
Prep Time: 10 minutes ⚭ *Cooking Time: 6 hours* ⚭ *Ideal slow-cooker size: 3½- or 4-qt.*

2 lbs. Brussels sprouts

¼ tsp. dried oregano

½ tsp. dried basil

2-oz. jar pimentos, drained

¼ cup, or 1 small can sliced black olives, drained

1 Tbsp. olive oil

½ cup water

1. Combine all ingredients in the slow cooker.

2. Cook on Low 6 hours, or until sprouts are just tender.

Calories: 70
Fat: 2.5g
Sodium: 60mg
Carbs: 11g
Sugar: 2.5g
Protein: 4g

Fresh Zucchini and Tomatoes

Pauline Morrison, St. Marys, Ontario

Makes 6–8 servings

Prep Time: 15 minutes   ⚘   Cooking Time: 2½–3 hours   ⚘   Ideal slow-cooker size: 3½-qt.

1½ lbs. zucchini, peeled if you wish, and cut into ¼" slices

19-oz. can low-sodium stewed tomatoes, broken up and undrained

1½ cloves garlic, minced

½ tsp. salt

1½ Tbsp. coconut oil

1. Place zucchini slices in the slow cooker.

2. Add tomatoes, garlic, and salt. Mix well.

3. Dot with coconut oil.

4. Cover and cook on High 2½–3 hours, or until zucchini are done to your liking.

Cal: 50
Fat: 3g
Sodium: 230mg
Carbs: 7g
Sugar: 5g
Protein: 2g

Garden Chips

MarJanita Geigley, Lancaster, PA

Makes 4 servings
Prep Time: 15 minutes ☘ Cooking Time: 2 hours ☘ Ideal slow-cooker size: 3- or 4-qt.

½ cup gluten-free rolled oats,
ground into flour

⅓ tsp. pepper

2 Tbsp. grated Parmesan cheese

3 egg whites

3–4 medium zucchini,
cut into ¼-inch slices

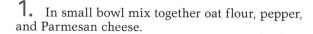

1. In small bowl mix together oat flour, pepper, and Parmesan cheese.

2. Place egg whites in another dish and whisk.

3. Dip zucchini in egg whites then into oat flour mixture.

4. Place zucchini into greased slow cooker and cook on Low for 1 hour.

5. Turn chips and cook for another hour.

Calories: 120
Fat: 2.5g
Sodium: 100mg
Carbs: 18g
Sugar: 4g
Protein: 8.5g

Corn on the Cob

Donna Conto, Saylorsburg, PA

Makes 3–4 servings
Prep Time: 10 minutes ❧ Cooking Time: 2–3 hours ❧ Ideal slow-cooker size: 5- or 6-qt.

6–8 ears of corn (in husk)
½ cup water

1. Remove silk from corn, as much as possible, but leave husks on.

2. Cut off ends of corn so ears can stand in the cooker.

3. Add water.

4. Cover. Cook on Low 2–3 hours.

Calories: 160
Fat: 2g
Sodium: 30mg
Carbs: 34g
Sugar: 6g
Protein: 6g

Eggplant Italian

Melanie Thrower, McPherson, KS

Makes 6–8 servings
Prep Time: 30 minutes ❧ *Cooking Time: 4 hours* ❧ *Ideal slow-cooker size: 4- or 5-qt. oval*

2 eggplants
¼ cup Egg Beaters
24 oz. fat-free cottage cheese
¼ tsp. salt
black pepper to taste
14-oz. can tomato sauce
2–4 Tbsp. Italian seasoning,
according to your taste preference

1. Peel eggplants and cut in ½-inch thick slices. Soak in salt water for about 5 minutes to remove bitterness. Drain well.

2. Spray slow cooker with fat-free cooking spray.

3. Mix Egg Beaters, cottage cheese, salt, and pepper together in bowl.

4. Mix tomato sauce and Italian seasoning together in another bowl.

5. Spoon a thin layer of tomato sauce into bottom of slow cooker. Top with about one-third of eggplant slices, and then one-third of egg/cheese mixture, and finally one-third of remaining tomato sauce mixture.

6. Repeat those layers twice, ending with seasoned tomato sauce.

7. Cover. Cook on High 4 hours. Allow to rest 15 minutes before serving.

Calories: 130
Fat: 1g
Sodium: 470mg
Carbs: 20g
Sugar: 9.5g
Protein: 13.5g

Side Dishes and Vegetables ❧ **265**

Slow-cooker Beets

Hope Comerford, Clinton Township, MI

Makes 4–6 servings
Prep Time: 10 minutes & Cooking Time: 3–4 hours & Ideal slow-cooker size: 3-qt.

4–6 large beets, scrubbed well and tops removed

3 Tbsp. olive oil

1 tsp. sea salt

¼ tsp. pepper

3 Tbsp. balsamic vinegar

1 Tbsp. lemon juice

1. Use foil to make a packet around each beet.

2. Divide the olive oil, salt, pepper, balsamic vinegar, and lemon juice evenly between each packet.

3. Place each beet packet into the slow cooker.

4. Cover and cook on Low for 3–4 hours, or until the beets are tender when poked with a knife.

5. Remove each beet packet from the crock and allow to cool and let the steam escape. Once cool enough to handle, use a paring knife to gently peel the skin off each beet. Cut into bite-sized pieces and serve with juice from the packet over the top.

Calories: 140
Fat: 8.5g
Sodium: 570mg
Carbs: 14.5g
Sugar: 10.5g
Protein: 2g

Baked Tomatoes

Lizzie Ann Yoder, Hartville, OH

Makes 4 servings
Prep Time: 10 minutes ⚬ *Cooking Time: 45 minutes–1 hour* ⚬ *Ideal slow-cooker size: 2½- or 3-qt.*

2 tomatoes, each cut in half

½ Tbsp. olive oil

½ tsp. parsley, chopped,
or ¼ tsp. dry parsley flakes

¼ tsp. dried oregano

¼ tsp. dried basil

1. Spray slow-cooker crock with nonfat cooking spray. Place tomato halves in crock.

2. Drizzle oil over tomatoes. Sprinkle with remaining ingredients.

3. Cover. Cook on High 45 minutes–1 hour.

Calories: 30
Fat: 2g
Sodium: 0mg
Carbs: 3.5g
Sugar: 2.5g
Protein: 1g

Mushrooms in Red Wine

Donna Lantgen, Chadron, NE

Makes 4 servings
Prep Time: 10 minutes ☘ *Baking Time: 4–6 hours* ☘ *Ideal slow-cooker size: 2-qt.*

1 lb. fresh mushrooms, cleaned
4 cloves garlic, chopped
¼ cup onion, chopped
1 Tbsp. olive oil
1 cup red wine

1. Combine all ingredients in the slow cooker. Cook on Low 4–6 hours, or until done to your liking.

2. Serve as a side dish with your favorite meat.

Cal: 120
Fat: 4g
Sodium: 25mg
Carbs: 8g
Sugar: 1g
Protein: 4g

Cabbage and Potatoes

Deb Kepiro, Strasburg, PA

Makes 4 servings

Prep Time: 15 minutes ☙ *Cooking Time: 3–6 hours* ☙ *Ideal slow-cooker size: 4-qt.*

1 small head green cabbage, sliced thinly

14 small red-skinned potatoes, cut in 1-inch chunks

1 small onion, diced

3 Tbsp. olive oil

2 Tbsp. balsamic vinegar

1 tsp. kosher salt

½ tsp. black pepper

1. Put all ingredients in the slow cooker. Mix well.

2. Cover and cook on High for 3 hours, until potatoes are as tender as you like them.

Calories: 570
Fat: 11g
Sodium: 720mg
Carbs: 108g
Sugar: 15.5g
Protein: 14g

Lemon Red Potatoes

Carol Leaman, Lancaster, PA

Makes 6 servings
Prep Time: 15–20 minutes ♣ Cooking Time: 2½–3 hours ♣ Ideal slow-cooker size: 3- to 4-qt.

10–12 small to medium-sized
red potatoes

¼ cup water

¼ cup coconut oil, melted

1 Tbsp. lemon juice

3 Tbsp. fresh or dried parsley

salt and pepper to taste

1. Cut a strip of peel from around the middle of each potato, using a potato peeler.

2. Place potatoes and water in the slow cooker.

3. Cover and cook on High 2½–3 hours, or until tender. Do not overcook.

4. Drain water.

5. Combine coconut oil, lemon juice, and parsley. Mix well. Pour over potatoes and toss to coat. Season with salt and pepper.

Cal: 180
Fat: 9g
Sodium: 30mg
Carbs: 24g
Sugar: 2g
Protein: 3g

Rosemary New Potatoes

Carol Shirk, Leola, PA

Makes 4–5 servings
Prep Time: 15 minutes ❧ *Cooking Time: 2–6 hours* ❧ *Ideal slow-cooker size: 3- to 4-qt.*

1½ lbs. new red potatoes, unpeeled

1 Tbsp. olive oil

1 Tbsp. fresh chopped rosemary, or 1 tsp. dried rosemary

1 tsp. garlic and pepper seasoning, or 1 large clove garlic, minced, plus ½ tsp. salt, and ¼ tsp. pepper

1. If the potatoes are larger than golf balls, cut them in half or in quarters.

2. In a bowl or plastic bag, toss potatoes with olive oil, coating well.

3. Add rosemary and garlic and pepper seasoning (or the minced garlic, salt, and pepper). Toss again until the potatoes are well coated.

4. Place potatoes in the slow cooker. Cook on High 2–3 hours, or on Low 5–6 hours, or until potatoes are tender but not mushy or dry.

Cal: 120
Fat: 3g
Sodium: 135mg
Carbs: 22g
Sugar: 2g
Protein: 3g

Garlicky Potatoes

Donna Lantgen, Chadron, NE

Makes 4–5 servings
Prep Time: 30 minutes   ♣   Cooking Time: 4½–6 hours   ♣   Ideal slow-cooker size: 3- to 4-qt.

6 potatoes, peeled and cubed

6 garlic cloves, minced

¼ cup diced onion, or one medium-sized onion, chopped

2 Tbsp. olive oil

1. Spray interior of slow cooker with nonstick cooking spray.

2. Combine all ingredients in the slow cooker.

3. Cover and cook on Low 4½–6 hours, or until potatoes are tender but not mushy or dry.

Cal: 170
Fat: 6g
Sodium: 25mg
Carbs: 27g
Sugar: 2g
Protein: 3g

Plain Old Scalloped Potatoes

Ruth Ann Penner, Hillsboro, KS

Makes 3–4 servings
Prep Time: 10 minutes ⚜ Cooking Time: 2 hours ⚜ Ideal slow-cooker size: 3-qt.

2 cups thinly sliced raw
potatoes, *divided*
1 Tbsp. gluten-free flour
1 tsp. salt
pepper (to taste)
1 cup milk
1 Tbsp. butter

1. Spray slow cooker with nonstick cooking spray.

2. Put half of thinly sliced potatoes in bottom of slow cooker.

3. In a small bowl, mix together flour, salt, and pepper. Sprinkle half over the potatoes.

4. Repeat layering.

5. Pour milk over all. Dot with butter.

6. Cover and cook on High for 2 hours.

TIPS

1. Pour milk over all as soon as possible to avoid having potatoes turn dark.

2. A cup of fully cooked ham cubes could be stirred in before serving.

3. Top with shredded cheese, if you wish.

Cal: 140
Fat: 5g
Sodium: 320mg
Carbs: 21g
Sugar: 4g
Protein: 4g

The Simplest "Baked" Potatoes

Donna Lantgen, Chadron, NE

Makes 4–5 servings

Prep Time: 30 minutes ⚬ *Cooking Time: 4½–6 hours* ⚬ *Ideal slow-cooker size: 3- to 4-qt.*

6 potatoes, peeled and cubed

6 garlic cloves, minced

¼ cup diced onion, or one medium-sized onion, chopped

2 Tbsp. olive oil

1. Spray interior of slow cooker with nonstick cooking spray.

2. Combine all ingredients in the slow cooker.

3. Cover and cook on Low 4½–6 hours, or until potatoes are tender but not mushy or dry.

Cal: 180
Fat: 6g
Sodium: 40mg
Carbs: 30g
Sugar: 2g
Protein: 4g

"Baked" Sweet Potatoes

Hope Comerford, Clinton Township, MI

Makes 5 potatoes
Prep Time: 2 minutes 🍂 Cooking Time: 4–5 hours 🍂 Ideal slow-cooker size: 5- or 6-qt.

5 sweet potatoes, pierced in several places with a fork or knife

1. Place sweet potatoes in the slow cooker.

2. Cover and cook on Low for 4–5 hours, or until they are tender when poked with a fork or knife.

Calories: 110
Fat: 0g
Sodium: 70mg
Carbs: 26g
Sugar: 5.5g
Protein: 2g

Quick and Light Sweet Potato Wedges

MarJanita Geigley, Lancaster, PA

Makes 4 servings
Prep Time: 15 minutes ❧ *Cooking Time: 3–5 hours* ❧ *Ideal slow-cooker size: 3-qt.*

4 sweet potatoes, cut into wedges
2 Tbsp. olive oil
2 tsp. Italian seasoning
3 Tbsp. light gluten-free Italian dressing
1 Tbsp. minced garlic

1. Combine all ingredients in sealable plastic bag and shake well.

2. Pour into the slow cooker and cook on Low for 3–5 hours.

Serving suggestion:

To make a dipping sauce, mix together Greek yogurt, Sriracha sauce, and minced garlic to taste.

Calories: 180
Fat: 7g
Sodium: 190mg
Carbs: 28.5g
Sugar: 6.5g
Protein: 2.5g

Thyme Roasted Sweet Potatoes

Hope Comerford, Clinton Township, MI

Makes 6 servings
Prep Time: 20 minutes   ⚜   Cooking Time: 2–3 hours   ⚜   Ideal slow-cooker size: 4-qt.

4–6 medium sweet potatoes, peeled, cubed

3 Tbsp. olive oil

5–6 large garlic cloves, minced

⅓ cup fresh thyme leaves

½ tsp. kosher salt

¼ tsp. red pepper flakes

1. Place all ingredients into the crock and stir.

2. Cover and cook on Low for 7 hours, or until potatoes are tender.

Calories: 160
Fat: 7g
Sodium: 250mg
Carbs: 23.5g
Sugar: 4.5g
Protein: 2g

Autumn Sweet Potatoes

Melinda Wenger, Middleburg, PA

Makes 4 servings

Prep Time: 20 minutes ⚬ *Cooking Time: 2–3 hours* ⚬ *Ideal slow-cooker size: 4-qt.*

4 medium sweet potatoes, peeled, sliced thinly

1 large Granny Smith apple, peeled and diced

½ cup raisins

zest and juice of ½ orange

2 Tbsp. maple syrup

toasted, chopped walnuts, for serving, *optional*

1. Place sweet potatoes in lightly greased slow cooker.

2. Top with apple, raisins, and orange zest. Drizzle with maple syrup and orange juice.

3. Cover and cook on High for 2–3 hours or until sweet potatoes are tender. Serve sprinkled with walnuts if you wish.

Calories: 230
Fat: 0g
Sodium: 75mg
Carbs: 56.5g
Sugar: 29g
Protein: 3g

Cooked Rice

Mary Kathryn Yoder, Harrisonville, MO

Makes 8 servings
Prep Time: 5 minutes ❧ Cooking Time: 1½–2½ hours ❧ Ideal slow-cooker size: 4-qt.

I Tbsp. butter
3 cups raw long-grain rice
6 cups water
salt to taste, about 3 tsp.

1. Grease slow cooker with the butter.

2. If you have time, heat the water to boiling in a saucepan on your stovetop, or in a microwave-safe bowl in your microwave. Then pour rice, water (heated or not), and salt into the cooker and stir together.

3. Cover and cook on High 1½–2½ hours. If you're home and able to do so, stir occasionally.

Calories: 265
Fat: 2g
Sodium: 430mg
Carbs: 55g
Sugar: 0g
Protein: 5g

Savory Rice

Jane Geigley, Lancaster, PA

Makes 6–8 servings
Prep Time: 10 minutes ❧ Cooking Time: 3–4 hours ❧ Ideal slow-cooker size: 4-qt.

2 cups uncooked short-grain
brown rice

5 cups water

1 Tbsp. coconut oil

½ tsp. ground thyme

2 Tbsp. dried parsley

2 tsp. garlic powder

1 tsp. dried basil

1 tsp. salt

1. Mix rice, water, coconut oil, thyme, parsley, garlic powder, basil, and salt.

2. Pour into the slow cooker. Cover.

3. Cook on High for 3–4 hours or until water is absorbed.

Calories: 230
Fat: 2.5g
Sodium: 340mg
Carbs: 46g
Sugar: 0g
Protein: 4g

Hometown Spanish Rice

Beverly Flatt-Getz, Warriors Mark, PA

Makes 6–8 servings
Prep Time: 20 minutes   Cooking Time: 2–4 hours   Ideal slow-cooker size: 4-qt.

1 large onion, chopped

1 bell pepper, chopped

1 lb. bacon, cooked, and broken into bite-sized pieces

2 cups cooked long-grain rice

28-oz. can low-sodium stewed tomatoes with juice

grated Parmesan cheese, *optional*

1. Sauté onion and pepper in a small nonstick frying pan until tender.

2. Spray interior of slow cooker with nonstick cooking spray.

3. Combine all ingredients in the slow cooker.

4. Cover and cook on Low 4 hours, or on High 2 hours, or until heated through.

5. Sprinkle with Parmesan cheese just before serving, if you wish.

Calories: 430
Fat: 23g
Sodium: 383mg
Carbs: 44g
Sugar: 4g
Protein: 12g

Aunt Twila's Beans

Mary Louise Martin, Boyd, WI

Makes 10–12 servings
Prep Time: 15 minutes ❧ *Cooking Time: 10 hours* ❧ *Ideal slow-cooker size: 5-qt.*

5 cups dry pinto beans
2 tsp. ground cumin
I medium yellow onion, minced
4 minced garlic cloves
9 cups water
3 tsp. salt
3 Tbsp. lemon juice

1. Combine beans, cumin, onion, garlic, and water in the slow cooker.

2. Cook on Low for 8 hours.

3. Add salt and lemon juice. Stir. Cook on Low for another 2 hours.

Calories: 310
Fat: 1g
Sodium: 650mg
Carbs: 56.5g
Sugar: 2.5g
Protein: 19g

Desserts and Beverages

Bananas Foster

Hope Comerford, Clinton Township, MI

Makes 6 servings
Prep Time: 5–10 minutes ⚜ Cooking Time: 1½–2 hours ⚜ Ideal slow-cooker size: 4-qt.

1 Tbsp. melted coconut oil

3 Tbsp. raw honey

3 Tbsp. fresh lemon juice

¼ tsp. cinnamon

dash of nutmeg

5 bananas (not green, but just yellow),
sliced into ½"-thick slices

1. Combine the first 5 ingredients in the crock.

2. Add the bananas in and stir to coat them evenly.

3. Cover and cook on Low for 1½–2 hours.

Calories: 140
Fat: 2.6g
Sodium: 2mg
Carbs: 32g
Sugar: 21g
Protein: 1g

Baked Apples

Marlene Weaver, Lititz, PA

Makes 4–6 servings

Prep Time: 10 minutes   ⚘   Cooking Time: 4 hours   ⚘   Ideal slow-cooker size: 6-qt.

2 Tbsp. raisins
¼ cup turbinado sugar
6–8 baking apples, cored
1 tsp. cinnamon
2 Tbsp. coconut oil
½ cup water

1. Mix raisins and sugar; fill center of apples.

2. Sprinkle with cinnamon and dot with coconut oil.

3. Place in the slow cooker; add water.

4. Cover and cook on Low for 4 hours.

Serving suggestion:

These apples are delicious with yogurt.

Calories: 189
Fat: 5g
Sodium: 3mg
Carbs: 36g
Sugar: 29g
Protein: 0g

Baked Apples with Dates

Mary E. Wheatley, Mashpee, MA

Makes 8 servings
Prep Time: 20–25 minutes ♣ Cooking Time: 2–6 hours
*Ideal slow-cooker size: 6-qt. oval, or large enough cooker that the apples
can each sit on the floor of the cooker, rather than being stacked*

8 medium-sized baking apples

Filling:
¾ cup coarsely chopped dates
3 Tbsp. chopped pecans
¼ cup honey

Topping:
1 tsp. ground cinnamon
½ tsp. ground nutmeg
1 Tbsp. coconut oil, melted
½ cup water

1. Wash, core, and peel top third of apples.

2. Mix dates and chopped nuts with honey. Stuff into centers of apples where cores had been.

3. Set apples upright in the slow cooker.

4. Sprinkle with cinnamon and nutmeg. Pour melted coconut oil evenly over each apple.

5. Add water around inside edge of cooker.

6. Cover. Cook on Low 4–6 hours or on High 2–3 hours, or until apples are as tender as you like them.

Calories: 70
Fat: 3.5g
Sodium: 0mg
Carbs: 11g
Sugar: 10.5g
Protein: .5g

Apple Appeal

Anne Townsend, Albuquerque, NM

Makes 6 servings
Prep Time: 10 minutes ❧ Cooking Time: 4–5 hours ❧ Ideal slow-cooker size: 3-qt.

6 baking apples, peeled, cored, and quartered

¼ tsp. nutmeg

2 Tbsp. turbinado sugar

¾ tsp. Asian five-spice powder

¼ cup apple juice

1. Place prepared apples in the slow cooker.

2. In a small mixing bowl, combine all remaining ingredients.

3. Pour into the slow cooker, stirring gently to coat apples.

4. Cover and cook on Low 4–5 hours, or until apples are as tender as you want them.

5. Serve the apples sliced or mashed, and warm, cold, or at room temperature.

6. These versatile apples may be served as a side dish with ham, scalloped potatoes, green beans amandine, cornbread, pecan tarts, or as a topping for toast!

Calories: 145
Fat: 0g
Sodium: 2mg
Carbs: 35g
Sugar: 28g
Protein: 0g

Chunky Applesauce

Hope Comerford, Clinton Township, MI

Makes 10 servings
Prep Time: 20 minutes ⚬ *Cooking Time: 6–8 hours* ⚬ *Ideal slow-cooker size: 3- or 4-qt.*

3 lbs. tart apples, peeled, cored, sliced
⅓ cup honey
½ cup water
1 tsp. lemon zest
3 Tbsp. lemon juice
3 cinnamon sticks

1. Spray the crock with nonstick spray.

2. Place all ingredients into the slow cooker. Stir to coat all apples.

3. Cover and cook on Low for 6–8 hours.

4. Remove cinnamon sticks and mash applesauce mixture lightly with a potato masher.

Calories: 100
Fat: 0g
Sodium: 0mg
Carbs: 28.5g
Sugar: 23.5g
Protein: .5g

Pears in Ginger Sauce

Sharon Timpe, Jackson, WI

Makes 6 servings

Prep Time: 20 minutes 🔸 Cooking Time: 3–5 hours 🔸 Standing Time: 45 minutes 🔸 Ideal slow-cooker size: 6-qt.

6 fresh pears with stems
1 cup white wine
⅓ cup honey
½ cup water
3 Tbsp. lemon juice
1 tsp. ground ginger
pinch nutmeg
pinch salt
¼ cup toasted coconut, for serving

1. Peel pears, leaving whole with stems intact.

2. Place pears in a greased slow cooker, upright, shaving bottoms slightly if necessary.

3. Combine wine, honey, water, lemon juice, ginger, nutmeg, and salt. Pour evenly over pears.

4. Cover and cook on Low for 3–5 hours, or until pears are tender.

5. Allow pears and liquid to cool.

6. To serve, set a pear in a dessert dish, drizzle with sauce, and sprinkle with toasted coconut.

Calories: 220
Fat: 5g
Sodium: 40mg
Carbs: 48g
Sugar: 33.5g
Protein: 1.44g

Quick Yummy Peaches

Willard E. Roth, Elkhart, IN

Makes 6 servings
Prep Time: 5–20 minutes ❧ Cooking Time: 5 hours ❧ Ideal slow-cooker size: 3-qt.

⅓ cup low-fat gluten-free baking mix

⅔ cup gluten-free oats

⅓ cup maple syrup

1 tsp. ground cinnamon

4 cups sliced fresh peaches

½ cup water

1. Mix together baking mix, oats, maple syrup, and cinnamon in a greased slow cooker.

2. Stir in peaches and water.

3. Cook on Low for at least 5 hours. (If you like a drier cobbler, remove lid for last 15–30 minutes of cooking.)

Calories: 140
Fat: 1g
Sodium: 60mg
Carbs: 33g
Sugar: 20g
Protein: 2g

Dates in Cardamom Coffee Syrup

Margaret W. High, Lancaster, PA

Makes 12 servings
Prep Time: 15 minutes ⚜ Cooking Time: 7–8 hours ⚜ Ideal slow-cooker size: 3-qt.

2 cups pitted, whole, dried dates

2½ cups very strong, hot brewed coffee

2 Tbsp. turbinado sugar

15 whole green cardamom pods

4-inch cinnamon stick

plain Greek yogurt, for serving

1. Combine dates, coffee, sugar, cardamom, and cinnamon stick in the slow cooker.

2. Cover and cook on High for 1 hour. Remove lid and continue to cook on high for 6–7 hours until sauce has reduced.

3. Pour dates and sauce into container and chill in fridge.

4. To serve, put a scoop of Greek yogurt in a small dish and add a few dates on top. Drizzle with a little sauce.

Calories: 80
Fat: 0g
Sodium: 0mg
Carbs: 20.5g
Sugar: 17.5g
Protein: .5g

Coconut Rice Pudding

Hope Comerford, Clinton Township, MI

Makes 6 servings
Prep Time: 5 minutes   ♣   Cooking Time: 2½ hours   ♣   Ideal slow-cooker size: 5- or 6-qt.

2½ cups low-fat milk
14-oz. can light coconut milk
½ cup turbinado sugar
1 cup arborio rice
1 stick cinnamon
1 cup dried cranberries, *optional*

1. Spray crock with nonstick spray.

2. In crock, whisk together the milk, coconut milk, and sugar.

3. Add in the rice and cinnamon stick.

4. Cover and cook on Low about 2–2½ hours, or until rice is tender and the pudding has thickened.

5. Remove cinnamon sticks. If using cranberries, sprinkle on top of each bowl of Coconut Rice Pudding.

Calories: 250
Fat: 4g
Sodium: 70mg
Carbs: 48g
Sugar: 22g
Protein: 4g

Slow-cooker Tapioca

Nancy W. Huber, Green Park, PA

Makes 12 servings
Prep Time: 10 minutes ⚜ Cooking Time: 3½ hours
Chilling Time: minimum 4 hours ⚜ Ideal slow-cooker size: 4-qt.

2 quarts fat-free milk

1 cup small pearl tapioca

½ cup honey

4 eggs, beaten

1 tsp. vanilla

fruit of choice, *optional*

1. Combine milk, tapioca, and honey in the slow cooker. Cook on High 3 hours.

2. Mix together eggs, vanilla, and a little hot milk from the slow cooker. Add to the slow cooker. Mix. Cook on High 20 more minutes.

3. Chill thoroughly, at least 4 hours. Serve with fruit.

Calories: 170
Fat: 1.5g
Sodium: 90mg
Carbs: 31g
Sugar: 20.5g
Protein: 7.5g

Dark Chocolate Lava Cake

Hope Comerford, Clinton Township, MI

Makes 8 servings

Prep Time: 5–10 minutes ⚶ *Cook Time: 2–3 hours* ⚶ *Ideal slow-cooker size: 4-qt.*

5 eggs

1 cup dark cocoa powder

⅔ cup maple syrup

⅔ cup dark chocolate, chopped into very fine pieces or shaved

1. Whisk the eggs together in a bowl and then slowly whisk in the remaining ingredients.

2. Spray the crock with nonstick spray.

3. Pour the egg/chocolate mixture into the crock.

4. Cover and cook on Low for 2–3 hours with some folded paper towel under the lid to collect condensation. It is done when the middle is set and bounces back up when touched.

Calories: 215
Fat: 10g
Sodium: 50mg
Carbs: 26g
Sugar: 17g
Protein: 7g

Dark Chocolate Peanut Butter Cocoa

Hope Comerford, Clinton Township, MI

Makes 10–12 servings
Prep Time: 5 minutes ⚶ *Cook Time: 5–6 hours* ⚶ *Ideal slow-cooker size: 3- or 4-qt.*

8 cups almond milk

½ cup powdered peanut butter

¼ cup turbinado sugar

12 oz. dark chocolate, broken into pieces

1 Tbsp. vanilla

1. Combine almond milk, powdered peanut butter, and turbinado sugar in crock.

2. Cover and cook low for 5–6 hours.

3. Stir in chocolate and vanilla until chocolate is melted, then serve.

Calories: 260
Fat: 13g
Sodium: 220mg
Carbs: 30g
Sugar: 25g
Protein: 7g

Home-Style Tomato Juice

Wilma Haberkamp, Fairbank, IA

Makes 4 cups

Prep Time: 20 minutes ⚜ Cooking Time: 4–6 hours ⚜ Ideal slow-cooker size: 3-qt.

10–12 large ripe tomatoes

1 tsp. salt

1 tsp. seasoned salt

¼ tsp. pepper

1 Tbsp. turbinado sugar

1. Wash and drain tomatoes. Remove core and blossom ends.

2. Place the whole tomatoes in your slow cooker. (Do not add water.)

3. Cover and cook on Low 4–6 hours, or until tomatoes are very soft.

4. Press them through a sieve or food mill.

5. Add seasonings. Chill.

TIP

If you have more than 10–12 tomatoes, you can use a larger slow cooker and double the recipe.

Calories: 41
Fat: 0g
Sodium: 350mg
Carbs: 9g
Sugar: 7g
Protein: 2g

Metric Equivalent Measurements

If you're accustomed to using metric measurements, I don't want you to be inconvenienced by the imperial measurements I use in this book.

Use this handy chart, too, to figure out the size of the slow cooker you'll need for each recipe.

Weight (Dry Ingredients)

1 oz		30 g
4 oz	¼ lb	120 g
8 oz	½ lb	240 g
12 oz	¾ lb	360 g
16 oz	1 lb	480 g
32 oz	2 lb	960 g

Slow Cooker Sizes

1-quart	0.96 l
2-quart	1.92 l
3-quart	2.88 l
4-quart	3.84 l
5-quart	4.80 l
6-quart	5.76 l
7-quart	6.72 l
8-quart	7.68 l

Volume (Liquid Ingredients)

½ tsp.		2 ml
1 tsp.		5 ml
1 Tbsp.	½ fl oz	15 ml
2 Tbsp.	1 fl oz	30 ml
¼ cup	2 fl oz	60 ml
⅓ cup	3 fl oz	80 ml
½ cup	4 fl oz	120 ml
⅔ cup	5 fl oz	160 ml
¾ cup	6 fl oz	180 ml
1 cup	8 fl oz	240 ml
1 pt	16 fl oz	480 ml
1 qt	32 fl oz	960 ml

Length

¼ in	6 mm
½ in	13 mm
¾ in	19 mm
1 in	25 mm
6 in	15 cm
12 in	30 cm

Recipe and Ingredient Index

About the Author

Hope Comerford is a mom, wife, elementary music teacher, blogger, recipe developer, public speaker, ALM Zone fit leader, Young Living Essential Oils essential oil enthusiast/educator, and published author. In 2013, she was diagnosed with a severe gluten intolerance and since then has spent many hours creating easy, practical, and delicious gluten-free recipes that can be enjoyed by both those who are affected by gluten and those who are not.

Growing up, Hope spent many hours in the kitchen with her Meme (grandmother), and her love for cooking grew from there. While working on her master's degree when her daughter was young, Hope turned to her slow cookers for some salvation and sanity. It was from there she began truly experimenting with recipes and quickly learned she had the ability to get a little more creative in the kitchen and develop her own recipes.

In 2010, Hope started her blog, *A Busy Mom's Slow Cooker Adventures*, to simply share the recipes she was making with her family and friends. She never imagined people all over the world would begin visiting her page and sharing her recipes with others as well. In 2013, Hope self-published her first cookbook, *Slow Cooker Recipes 10 Ingredients or Less and Gluten-Free*, and then later wrote *The Gluten-Free Slow Cooker*.

Hope became the new brand ambassador and author of Fix-It and Forget-It in mid-2016. Since then, she has brought her excitement and creativeness to the Fix-It and Forget-It brand. Through Fix-It and Forget-It, she has written *Fix-It and Forget-It Lazy & Slow, Fix-It and Forget-It Healthy Slow Cooker Cookbook, Fix-It and Forget-It Favorite Slow Cooker Recipes for Mom, Fix-It and Forget-It Favorite Slow Cooker Recipes for Dad, Fix-It and Enjoy-It Welcome Home Cookbook, Fix-It and Forget-It Holiday Favorites, Fix-It and Forget-It Cooking for Two, Fix-It and Forget-It Crowd Pleasers for the American Summer, Fix-It and Forget-It Dump Dinners and Dump Desserts, Welcome Home Diabetic Cookbook, Welcome Home Harvest Cookbook, Fix-It and Forget-It Instant Pot Cookbook,* and *Fix-It and Forget-It Freezer Meals.*

Hope lives in the city of Clinton Township, Michigan, near Metro Detroit. She is a native of Michigan and has lived there her whole life. She has been happily married to her husband and best friend, Justin, since 2008. Together they have two children, Ella and Gavin, who are her motivation, inspiration, and heart. In her spare time, Hope enjoys traveling, singing, cooking, reading books, spending time with friends and family, and relaxing.

FIX-IT and FORGET-IT®